REVELATION

A Book for the Rest of Us

*   *   *

Can Down-to-Earth Christians Affirm
John's Heavenly Visions
as True and Helpful?

REVELATION

A Book for the Rest of Us

by

Scott Gambrill Sinclair

*   *   *

BIBAL Press
P.O. Box 11123
Berkeley, CA 94701-2123

Revelation: A Book for the Rest of Us

Library of Congress Cataloging-in-Publication Data

Sinclair, Scott Gambrill, 1950 – .
    Revelation : a book for the rest of us / Scott Gambrill Sinclair.
      p. cm.
    ISBN 0-941037-19-3 : $12.95
    1. Bible. N.T. Revelation--Criticism, interpretation, etc.
  I. Title.
  BS2825.2.S573   1992
  228'.06--dc20
                                 92-8748
                                     CIP

Published by BIBAL Press
Berkeley, CA 94701

Dedicated to my students at Codrington College, Barbados,

in thanksgiving for their love and support

TABLE OF CONTENTS

Preface .... Page 9

Part I: A Critique of Various Approaches to Interpreting Revelation

Chapter 1: Some Problems with the Usual Approaches
to Revelation 15

Chapter 2: Revelation's Inclusion in the Bible as an
Implicit Criticism of the Usual Approaches 23

Chapter 3: Five Possible Ways to Interpret Biblical Prophecy 29

Chapter 4: The Necessity and Difficulty of the Five Ways
in Interpreting Revelation 37

***Part II: Revelation's Historical Background and Literary Structure
and Its Original Message***

Chapter 5: Revelation's Old Testament and Intertestamental
Background and Its Significance 45

Chapter 6: Revelation's Social Setting 51

Chapter 7: The Basic Structure of Revelation
and Its Significance 59

Chapter 8: The Basic Message of Revelation 73

Part III: The Spiritual Basis of Revelation's Message

Chapter 9: John's Invitation to Judge His Visions
From the Inside 81

Chapter 10: The Nature of God and the Deeds of the Lamb 87

Chapter 11: The Nature of Evil and Our Hope
of the New Jerusalem 95

Chapter 12: The Origin of John's Visions 105

Part IV: Is Revelation True?

Chapter 13: How Do We Determine a Document Is True? 113

Chapter 14: The Truth of Revelation as a Visionary Prophecy 117

Chapter 15: The Truth of Revelation as a Christian Document 125

Chapter 16: The Truth of Revelation as a Work of Art 131

Part V: Is Revelation Helpful?

Chapter 17: The Positive Contribution of Revelation
to the Canon 137

Chapter 18: The Contribution of Revelation to
Christian Art and Worship 143

Chapter 19: The Value of Revelation for
Contemporary Spirituality 147

Chapter 20: The Positive Contribution of Revelation to Living
in a World that Is in Danger of Destroying Itself 153

Preface

Some books on Revelation provide us primarily with technical information. These books spend the bulk of their space dealing with historical or literary questions such as, "What is the literary structure of Revelation?" or, "What was going on when Revelation was written?"

Other books on Revelation provide us with forecasts. These books take material from Revelation and use it to predict what will happen in the next few years.

What you are holding in your hands, however, was written for the rest of us. By "the rest of us," I mean Christians who find Revelation powerful or problematic, but who are not especially interested in purely historical and literary matters and who are suspicious of detailed prophecies of the future, regardless of whether these are based on the stars or the Bible. By "the rest of us," I mean Christians who want to believe that a major book of the New Testament is comprehensible and true, but who, quite frankly, see Revelation as simply weird or false or both. By "the rest of us," I mean people whose primary concern in reading Revelation is to get something out of it that will enrich their present relationship to God and other Christians, something that will help them see the world with new wisdom and live with new joy.

In writing that this book is for "the rest of us," I do not wish to suggest there is nothing here that could interest persons who are concerned about technical matters or who rely on Revelation to predict future events. I hope biblical specialists will find my book informative, since it does offer suggestions on a number of literary and historical issues. Similarly, I hope that people who use Revelation to predict the future will find this book challenging. It is my conviction that Revelation does not give us specific knowledge of upcoming events, and I will try to show that attempts to use the book to forecast what will soon take place are counterproductive. I hope that people who disagree with me will at least take the trouble of considering an opposing position.

In writing that this book is for "the rest of us," what I mean to emphasize is that it will struggle with the most basic question about Revelation (or any Christian work), namely: Is it true, and, if so, how does this truth help me and my Christian community? This book has five sections. In the first I will critique different approaches to interpreting Revelation. In the second we will discuss its historical background, literary form, and original meaning. In the third we will examine the spiritual basis of Revelation's message. Then in the fourth and fifth we will deal respectively with the issues of whether that message is true and whether it is helpful.

This book is especially intended to serve as an alternative textbook for an introductory course on Revelation. It in fact contains the substance of lectures I gave on the Apocalypse at Codrington College, Barbados. Most of the chapters roughly correspond to individual lectures, though I have made significant changes.

As befits a textbook, I have included discussions of some technical issues, but I do not think that general readers will find these discussions too distracting. No serious study of a biblical book can dispense with technical discussions altogether. However, I have tried to keep them as brief and simple as possible. I have avoided the use of specialized terminology whenever feasible and kept footnotes to a minimum. People who have not taken a college or seminary class on Revelation may find parts of this book challenging. I believe, however, that any educated person who has a reasonable knowledge of the Bible and especially Revelation, will find what I have written comprehensible. I also hope they will find it a blessing.

I would like to thank a number of people and institutions for their help. First of all, I gratefully acknowledge the hospitality of Codrington College, Barbados, where for four years I gave the lectures on which this book is based and the hospitality of the Church Divinity School of the Pacific where I spent time writing the actual text. I also am grateful to a number of individuals for reading drafts of the book and making various suggestions: Prof. Duane Christensen, Mr. Ronald Culmer, Dr. Robert Dietel, Ms. Nancy Evans, Prof. Donald Gelpi, S.J., Dean Sherman Johnson, Ms. Deidre Jordy, Prof. John Kater, The Rev. Peter Michaelson, Prof. Donn Morgan, Ms. Carole Robinson, and Ms. Jan Robitscher. Without the help of these intelligent and perceptive counselors, this would be a much poorer book. Since I did not always heed their advice, however, I am solely responsible for the defects that remain. Ms. M.R. Ritley provided valuable computer assistance. My mother and my brother Winfield and his wife Julie allowed me to live for long periods free of charge at their houses while I worked on these pages. Finally, as I complete writing, I cannot help thinking of Fr. John R. Keating, S.J. It was Fr. Keating who taught the first course I took on Revelation, now nearly two decades ago. During that course I began struggling with the issues that so many years later were to be the subject of this book.

The translations from the Greek New Testament are my own and are based on the Third Edition of the text published by the United Bible Societies.

PART I

A Critique of Various Approaches
to Interpreting Revelation

Chapter 1

Some Problems
with the Usual Approaches to Revelation

And I will grant to my two witnesses that they may prophesy one
thousand two hundred sixty days dressed in sackcloth. These are
the two olive trees and the two lampstands which stand before the
Lord of the earth. And if anyone wants to harm them, fire goes
out from their mouth and eats up their enemies; and if anyone
would wish to harm them, so that one must be killed. These have
the authority to lock the heavens so that rain may not fall for the
days of their prophecy, and they have authority over the waters to
turn them into blood and to strike the earth with every blow, as
often as they want. And when they finish their testimony, the
beast that is ascending from the abyss will make war with them
and will conquer them and kill them. And their corpse will be on
the main street of the Great City which is, spiritually speaking,
called "Sodom" and "Egypt," where also their Lord was crucified.
And members from peoples and tribes and tongues and nations
look at their corpse for three and a half days, and they do not let
their corpses be put into a tomb. And those who dwell on the
earth rejoice over them and celebrate, and they will send gifts to
one another, because these two prophets tormented those who
dwell on the earth. And after the three and a half days a spirit of
life from God entered into them, and they stood upon their feet,
and great fear fell upon those who watched them. And they
heard a great voice from heaven saying to them, "Come up here!"
And they went up into heaven in the cloud, and their enemies
watched them. And in that hour there was a great earthquake,
and a tenth of the city fell, and in the earthquake seven thousand
persons were killed, and the rest became terrified and gave glory
to the God of heaven. (Rev. 11:3-13)

Except for Revelation, the books of the New Testament present a
world that is basically familiar and thus relatively easy to understand.

Like our own, the world of the gospels and epistles is one which has altars and sheep, cities and seas. To be sure, within the basic similarity there are significant differences. Unlike most places today, ancient altars were used for animal sacrifices; ancient sheep were kept in small groups tended by individual shepherds; ancient cities lacked such things as cars and skyscrapers; and the ancient sea had not yet been tamed by modern nautical advances. Yet the fundamental reality was much the same. As a result, it is relatively easy for us even to make sense of the differences. We have little problem understanding an ancient altar, because it was basically similar to a modern one except that animal sacrifices were offered on it; or understanding the ancient sea, because it was like the modern except that it had not yet been tamed.

Because the world of the gospels and epistles is familiar, there has usually been agreement at the most elementary level on how these books are to be interpreted. Of course, there have been innumerable debates concerning details. Yet, at the most basic level, readers have always concurred on what these books mean. No one doubts that Paul was a human being rather than an animal or that Jesus was crucified in Jerusalem rather than Rome.

By contrast, the Book of Revelation presents a world that is basically alien. To be sure, like our own, Revelation's world also contains altars and sheep, cities and sea. Yet here the similarity ends, for these common elements are themselves fundamentally different. In Revelation an altar can talk (Rev. 16:7); a lamb can have seven horns and seven eyes (Rev. 5:6); a city can be made of pure, transparent gold (Rev. 21:18); and the sea can turn into blood (Rev. 16:3).

As a result, even at the most fundamental level it is often far from obvious what the book means. We may illustrate the ambiguities by considering the two witnesses described in Rev. 11:3-13. Despite all the pictorial details that the text gives us, it is by no means evident whether these "two olive trees" and "lampstands" are human beings or not or whether the Great City in which they are killed, which is "called 'Sodom' and 'Egypt,'" is Jerusalem or Rome.

The problem of interpreting Revelation is further aggravated by the fact that the book claims to predict future events (e.g., Rev. 1:1). When we are dealing with the past or the present, we know basically what the world was (or is) like. As a result, it is easy to distinguish the real from the imaginary, and we seldom have difficulty deciding whether something is a news story or a fairy tale. Unfortunately, however, we cannot be certain what the future will be like even at the most basic level. It is at least possible that tomorrow the world will be fundamentally different (due to a nuclear war, for instance). Moreover, if someone had been able to describe modern technology to citizens of the era in which Revelation was written, I suspect they would have dismissed our world as a fairy tale.

Because Revelation is so obscure, speculative Christians down through the ages have been able to read their own prejudices into the text. Highly polarized believers have again and again sought to prove that their hated opponents somehow fit the number "666" and so were in reality the nefarious monster described in Revelation 13 (the actual number occurs in verse 18). For example, in the Middle Ages, Franciscan opponents of Pope Benedict XI pointed out that in Greek (where letters also stand for numbers) the sum of the letters of "Benedict" comes to 666.[1] Of course, there has been no shortage of other candidates. One scholar writes,[2]

> The antitype of the Beast, or of Antichrist, in accordance with the time, place, and persuasion of the interpreter, has been variously identified as the Jews, the Ottomans, the Pope, France, Charles I, Cromwell, priestcraft, the alliance against revolutionary France, the landholding aristocracy, capitalists, the American slaveholder, and Hitler.

Another equally popular pastime with would-be prophets has been using Revelation (perhaps in combination with other books) to predict the date of the millennium. Sometimes such predictions have been so widely believed that whole societies became inflamed with hope or terror. In the late Middle Ages many thought the millennium would arrive in the year 1260. As a result, when the year came, there was widespread hysteria in Italy, including an "outbreak of mass self-flagellation."[3] In Reformation England some thought that 1666 was the divinely appointed date. Consequently, "from 1660 on, there was a spate of fresh speculation on the signs of the times, the arrival of the beast, the coming of Armageddon, and similar events."[4] As I was thinking about writing this book, I happened to read in a newspaper that "many modern-day prophets" are suggesting that the year 2000 is about the right time.[5] It is, however, too soon to know whether this prediction will also lead to mass frenzy.

The speculative use of Revelation has, of course, attractive features. To begin with, futuristic exegesis makes the book obviously relevant. Once one concludes that Revelation proves that one's present enemy is the Antichrist or that the end of all things is at hand, the book becomes singularly interesting and important. To quote from the opening of Hal Lindsey's popular commentary, Revelation becomes "more up-to-date than tomorrow's newspaper!"[6] Another strength of futuristic exegesis is that it inspires burning hope. Perhaps nothing brings the same relief and joy — especially to people who have little in this world to hope for — as the conviction that soon the Lamb will come, and his elect will reign on earth or enter into the New Jerusalem. Because futuristic exegesis makes the book obviously relevant and inspires burning hope, it also recaptures some of the impact that Revelation must have had, and was intended to have, when it first appeared. As we shall see later, Revelation itself identified the church's enemies of the day as the various beasts, and it intended to give its readers the enlivening expectation that their final deliverance would be soon. As a result, futuristic commentaries on the Apocalypse allow the reader to experience at least some of the power that the book once possessed. Hence, the common criticism that speculative commentaries are untrue to the Apocalypse is at best itself only a half-truth. In many ways Hal Lindsey's popular works give the reader a much better sense of what Revelation is really about than do, for example, the erudite volumes of R. H. Charles.[7]

Still, speculative interpretations of the book suffer from a besetting problem: Attempts to correlate present and future events with the predictions of the Apocalypse have always failed. Each century has read its own situation into Revelation's provocative pages, and each century's exegesis has, at least in retrospect, seemed to lack a real foundation either in the text or in any divine plan. Thus, in the early seventeenth century Thomas Brightman explained that the first three vials (Rev. 16:2-7) referred to events in the previous half century in his own England. The first vial occurred in 1563 when Elizabeth I dismissed papist clergy; the second occurred in 1564 when the Council of Trent reaffirmed Catholic doctrinal errors; and the third occurred in 1581 when the English Parliament passed an act "against the treason of papists."[8] Four centuries later it is almost unimaginable that these events could be what the vials in question referred to or are some of the final plagues immediately preceding the consummation of the world. Yet contemporary speculative commentators place great emphasis on events in our own day that in a later century may well seem equally inappropriate as interpretative tools to unlock either the Apocalypse or God's final intentions. Of course, contemporary commentators assure us that we can have more confidence in these new predictions because now the events of the end time are beginning, and so we finally have the data that makes the apocalypse comprehensible and credible. Thus, Lindsey quoting Scofield declares, "The book [Revelation] is so written that as the actual time of these events approach, the current events will unlock the meaning of the book."[9] It is, however, at least sobering that in previous centuries other commentators made similar claims.[10]

The failure of past interpretations is especially serious because often it led either to disillusionment or dishonesty. The problem is not merely that the divine fulfillment did not come in the year 1260 or 1666 or whenever; the problem is that in many cases burning expectation was disappointed. Unfortunately, when hope proves false, the price is high. Indeed, one has only two options in the face of such disappointment. One can surrender the hope itself and so lose confidence in God's plan, or else one can indulge in hypocrisy and pretend that really nothing serious went wrong. In my opinion, the second option is even more questionable than the first. As nearly as I can tell, it has also been more common. In the eighteenth century William Whiston (the translator of Josephus) predicted that the millennium would begin in 1715; then, when that year came and went, he settled on 1734; after that prediction also failed, he wisely chose a year which was bound to be long after his own demise, namely 1866.[11] In our own century Hal Lindsey prophesied that the events of the end time would occur within a biblical generation of 1948, the year of the (re)founding of the Jewish state. Moreover, Lindsey explicitly stated that a biblical generation was around forty years.[12] Subsequently, when things did not turn out as expected, he explained in an interview that a generation might be sixty to eighty years.[13]

Beyond the disillusionment and dishonesty that futuristic predictions have inspired, one must also ask whether these predictions have been true to the spirit of New Testament teaching. The gospels suggest that on the whole Jesus was opposed to seeking signs. According to Matthew, he insisted that it is an "evil and adulterous generation" that seeks signs and that to such a generation no sign would be given (Matt. 12:39). To be sure, the apocalyptic discourses (Mark 13 and parallels), that, I believe, reflect later church theology, provide a catalogue of signs.

Yet even in these passages the New Testament insists that no one can know the day or the hour (Mark 13:32; parallel Matt. 24:36). Radical interpreters often give all this theology lip service by holding that no one can know the exact time but that we can discover the approximate one. Yet it seems to me that people like Lindsey in fact do what the New Testament attacks.

Finally, one must ask whether many futuristic treatments of Revelation have needlessly inflamed hatred and fear, with incalculable historical consequences. As we noted above, it has been a common practice to brand one's enemy of the moment as the Antichrist. To some extent such identification only reflects enmity and anxiety that exist already. Yet such identification naturally leads to an increase of polarization. Almost by definition, the final enemy of God is supremely loathsome and terrifying, and once one decides someone else is the Beast, it is only natural to loathe them even more. The historical consequences of this heightened animosity have been grim. One scholar writes

> Such thinking has helped engender a collective paranoia, religious or racial or national, which has manifested itself in Crusades, sacred wars, pogroms, witch-hunts, or other attempts to achieve, by annihilating the massed forces of evil, a final solution.[14]

Because Revelation is obscure and because speculative thinkers have made such bad use of it, circumspect thinkers in the church have down through the ages tended to ignore or dismiss the book. Of course, since Revelation was part of holy writ, orthodox Christians could not attack it outright. What they could and did do was to leave it alone. Writing in the Renaissance, the great Christian humanist scholar Erasmus noted, "Ancient theologians quote passages from this book rather for illustration and ornament than for support of a serious proposition."[15] In the Enlightenment Reimarus made essentially the same point, but, as befits an enemy of the church, he was less polite: "Reasonable theologians prefer to refrain from the seven sealed book and confess that of all its wonderful visions they cannot with certainty interpret a single one."[16]

Since that time, the situation has basically remained the same. To be sure, our knowledge of what Revelation meant when it was written has increased, and there has been a continuing sense that we ought to do something with the Apocalypse. Technical commentaries have proliferated, and we have seen some popular treatments on the value of Revelation. Sadly, however, the technical commentaries usually include only the briefest reflections on whether the book is useful today, and the popular discussions on Revelation's value seem content to affirm that the book is Christian or contains things that are helpful. What we never find is a systematic discussion of *whether Revelation is actually true and, if so, how that truth contributes something to Christianity which otherwise would be missing.* Consequently, mainline scholarship simply has not succeeded in making the work theologically significant. Despite all the technical progress and the best of intentions, what Erasmus said remains true today: In serious theology the book is used primarily for illustration and ornament.

Notes

[1]The suggestion was published by Ubertino di Casale. See R. H. Charles, "History of the Interpretation of the Apocalypse," in *Studies in the Apocalypse* (Edinburgh: T. & T. Clark, 1913), pp. 20-21.

[2]M. H. Abrams, "Apocalypse: Theme and Variations," in C. A. Patrides and Joseph Wittreich, eds., *The Apocalypse in English Renaissance Thought and Literature: Patterns, Antecedents, and Repercussions* (Ithaca: Cornell University Press, 1984), p. 353.

[3]Norman Cohn, *The Pursuit of the Millennium: Revolutionary Millenarians and Mystical Anarchists of the Middle Ages* (London: Temple Smith, rev. ed., 1970), p. 128.

[4]Paul J. Korshin, "Queuing and Waiting: The Apocalypse in England, 1660-1750," in *The Apocalypse in English Renaissance Thought*, p. 252.

[5]"Armageddon Fever," *The Birmingham News*, Sunday, August 12, 1990, pp. 1, 5A.

[6]Hal Lindsey, *There's A New World Coming: A Prophetic Odyssey* (Santa Ana: Vision House, 1973), p. 15.

[7]In many ways the two volume commentary by R. H. Charles still remains the standard work on Revelation, even though it is now more than half a century old. See R. H. Charles, *A Critical and Exegetical Commentary on the Revelation of St. John* (New York: Scribner's, 1920).

[8]Katherine R. Firth, *The Apocalyptic Tradition in Reformation Britain, 1530-1645* (Oxford: Oxford University Press, 1979), p. 170.

[9]Lindsey, *There's a New World*, p. 21.

[10]For a similar statement by John Napier from the late sixteenth century, see Firth, *Apocalyptic Tradition*, p. 148.

[11]Charles, *Studies*, p. 39.

[12]Hal Lindsey with C. C. Carlson, *The Late Great Planet Earth* (Grand Rapids: Zondervan, 1970), pp. 43, 54. It should be noted that this particular prediction was not based on Revelation.

[13]*Christianity Today*, April 15, 1977, p. 40. I first learned about this interview through Dewey M. Beegle, *Prophecy and Prediction* (Ann Arbor: Pryor Pettengill, 1978), p. 214.

[14]M. H. Abrams, "Apocalypse: Theme and Variations," in *The Apocalypse in English Renaissance Thought*, p. 346.

[15]Quoted in Firth, *Apocalyptic Tradition*, p. 8.

[16]Quoted in Charles, *Studies*, p. 46.

Chapter 2

Revelation's Inclusion in the Bible as an Implicit Criticism of the Usual Approaches

The primary reason Revelation is so important to Christians is that it is *in the Bible* and thus authoritative. Christians are, of course, free to ignore or dismiss such things as newspaper editorials or astrology columns. We do not have the same freedom to ignore or dismiss a major book of the New Testament. Thus, even though circumspect theologians down through the ages would have liked to forget about Revelation, they still used it for illustration and ornament. They did so because Scripture could not simply be set aside. Similarly, one reason speculators have such confidence in analyses and predictions based on the Apocalypse is that Revelation is the *Word of God* and so, properly understood, must be true. Indeed, it is noteworthy that often futuristic and polemical commentators make the sharpest possible distinction between what they do and the occult, even though on the basis of content such a distinction is dubious. Thus, Lindsey repeatedly castigates such things as astrology and even links the occult to the coming of the Antichrist.[1] Yet, if we concentrate on Lindsey's predictions themselves and ignore their biblical foundation, they seem far more arbitrary and fantastic than anything in the daily astrology columns.

Accordingly, it is important to discover what the ancient church had in mind when it put Revelation in the New Testament. If Revelation is authoritative for Christians primarily because it is in the Bible, then ultimately its authority stems from that series of historical decisions that led to its inclusion in the New Testament canon. Hence, if only we can discern why the Christian community made the Apocalypse part of scripture, we would have some guidelines to tell us how to interpret the book. We could also insist that certain interpreters do not have the right to appeal to the book's biblical status if they use the Apocalypse in ways that those who put it in the Bible found objectionable.

Significantly, no canonical book of scripture had as much difficulty getting into the New Testament as did Revelation. Here we will not try to review the history of the formation of the New Testament canon, since a number of excellent histories already exist.[2] Instead, we will merely cite some of the most relevant and striking data regarding the problems Revelation had getting accepted. At various times and places in early church history important individuals and groups opposed (or at least questioned) Revelation's right to be in the scriptures. In the late second or early third century Gaius and the so-called Alogoi explicitly rejected Revelation along with the other Johannine writings.[3] In the early fourth century Eusebius diplomatically placed Revelation in his list of universally accepted books *and* in his list of disputed ones and in both places added the qualifying phrase "if it seems desirable" (*Eccles. Hist.*, 3.25). In the subsequent centuries the debate over whether Revelation should be in the canon continued, and at least most of the Eastern Church rejected the Apocalypse. For example, Amphilochius of Iconium (d. after 394) noted that while some people approved of Revelation, most held that it was spurious.[4] Apparently Amphilochius himself sided with the latter party.

As a result of such continuing opposition, Revelation was the last book of the New Testament to be generally recognized as canonical. It is especially striking that many ancient New Testaments are identical to our own *except for the absence of Revelation.* Perhaps the first list of the New Testament canon that is identical to the present one is the one contained in some manuscripts of Origen's *Homilies on Joshua* (vii. 1).[5] Yet it is noteworthy that most manuscripts of this work omit Revelation. Apparently then, Origen or his future scribes regarded all our present New Testament other than the Apocalypse as canonical.[6] Many subsequent lists of New Testament writings are identical to the modern apart from the omission of Revelation. The writings of Cyril of Jerusalem (*Catachesis* iv. 36), Gregory of Nazianzus, and the decree of the Synod of Laodicea[7] all have our New Testament canon except that Revelation is missing. Perhaps most impressive of all is the manuscript evidence. As of 1980 there were only 59 known manuscripts of the complete Greek New Testament. However, there were 149 of the entire Greek New Testament minus the Apocalypse.[8] Only in the Middle Ages was Revelation more or less universally accepted.

One important reason that Revelation was so often excluded from the canonical books was widespread doubt concerning its apostolic authorship. Again and again, Christian scholars expressed well-justified doubt over whether the author of John's Gospel could also be the author of the Apocalypse. Thus, Gaius and the Alogoi attributed Revelation to the Gnostic Cerinthus.[9] In the third century Dionysius, bishop of Alexandria, in a triumph of ancient biblical scholarship, conclusively demonstrated on the basis of style, content, and the actual claims of the documents themselves that the writer of Revelation could not be that of the other Johannine books[10] (Eusebius, *Eccles. Hist.* 7.25). Subsequently, those who opposed the inclusion of Revelation in the canon questioned its apostolic authorship. Thus, Eusebius attributed the book to John the Elder, rather than John the Apostle (*Eccles. Hist.* 3.39.5-6).

Yet it seems that the authorship of the book was not the primary issue—the real reason Christians so often rejected the book was that Revelation was obscure and its obscurity encouraged irresponsible speculation. Here the remarks of Dionysius about the earlier history of the discussion are singularly informative:[11]

> Some indeed of those before our time rejected and altogether impugned the book, examining it chapter by chapter and declaring it to be unintelligible and illogical, and its title false. For they say that it is not John's, no, nor yet an apocalypse [unveiling], since it is veiled by its heavy, thick curtain of unintelligibility; and that the author of this book was not only not one of the apostles, nor even one of the saints or those belonging to the Church, but Cerinthus, the same who created the sect called "Cerinthian" after him, since he desired to affix to his own forgery a name worthy of credit. For that this was the doctrine which he taught, that the kingdom of Christ would be on earth; and he dreamed that it would consist in those things which formed the object of his own desires. (Eusebius, *Eccles. Hist.* 7.25.1-3)

These words make it clear that authorship was not the real concern of the earliest critics. Their real concern was that the enigmatic contents of the book allowed irresponsible thinkers to justify strange and dubious doctrines. Dionysius' concern was the same. He only investigated the authorship of the Apocalypse after he discovered that some people in his diocese were using the book to justify belief in a literal thousand-year reign of the saints on earth (Eusebius, *Eccles. Hist.* 7.24).

In the end the church agreed to canonize Revelation, but only with the understanding that the book was not to be used for speculation. In the Western church the price for inclusion in the New Testament was in the end set by Augustine of Hippo. It was Augustine who attended three crucial provincial synods in the late fourth and early fifth centuries and successfully lobbied for the present New Testament.[12] In his writings Augustine took pains to insure that Revelation would not be used for futuristic speculation. He insisted that what Revelation meant by the first resurrection was the entrance into the Christian life through baptism (*City of God* XX.6-7) and that what Revelation meant by the thousand-year reign of the saints on earth was the history of the church (*City of God* XX.6, 9). He also held that the final events described in Revelation would not occur any time soon. Subsequently, Augustine's conservative interpretation was extraordinarily influential in the West. In the East the price of acceptance was allegorization. The images of the Apocalypse were taken to be symbols of timeless truth, not predictions of the future. Once again Dionysius is informative. Despite his conclusions about the book's authorship, he continued to regard Revelation as Scripture. However, he insisted that the book must not be understood literally (Eusebius, *Eccles. Hist.* 7.24.4-6). In this approach Dionysius was simply reflecting what apparently had already become standard in Alexandrian scholarship. It seems Alexandrian theologians normally resorted to allegorical exegesis to counter futuristic interpretations of Revelation. Indeed, in his investigation of the millenarian movement in his diocese, Dionysius discovered that the millenarians revered a book entitled *Refutation of the Allegorists* (Eusebius, *Eccles. Hist.* 7.24). The allegorical approach has continued to dominate much Christian scholarship until modern times.

The history of Revelation's entry into the New Testament canon suggests two contrasting perspectives. On the one hand, Revelation is a work of momentous importance. In the end the church, despite all of its often well-justified doubts, canonized the work. Canonization, of course, was the highest possible honor the church could bestow on a document and indicated that the work in question was all but indispensable to Christian life and faith. On the one hand Revelation was not to be an invitation for futuristic speculation. Yet, the price of canonization was the exclusion of millenarian exegesis.

These perspectives implicitly challenge the beliefs of the conservatives and speculators down through the ages. The perspective that Revelation is of momentous importance to Christian life and faith challenges the conservative tendency to ignore or, at least, to marginalize the work. Surely the church would never have included Revelation in the canon if the book was only for illustration and ornament! The perspective that Revelation is not to be used for speculation undermines the attempts to appeal to the book's authority to justify fanciful predictions. The book's authority came from Christian leaders who insisted Revelation must not be used for futuristic speculation. Hence, commentators like Hal Lindsey are not entitled to assume that Revelation is part of the Bible. The book became part of the Bible only after it was decided that the work would not be used for speculation. Commentators who ignore this decision are themselves under the obligation to demonstrate that the book is inspired and in particular that it is inspired as a detailed chronicle of coming events.

Notes

[1] E.g., Hal Lindsey, *There's A New World Coming: A Prophetic Odyssey* (Santa Ana: Vision House, 1973), pp. 144-146.

[2] A recent example is Bruce M. Metzger, *The Canon of the New Testament: Its Origin, Development, and Significance* (Oxford: Clarendon Press, 1987). Most of the data in the remainder of this chapter comes from Metzger.

[3] The relevant texts can be found in Robert M. Grant, *Second-Century Christianity: A Collection of Fragments* (London: SPCK, 1946), pp. 105-108.

[4] For a translation of the relevant section of the text, see Metzger, *Canon*, pp. 313-314.

[5] For the text, see Metzger, *Canon*, p. 139.

[6] Metzger, *Canon*, p. 139. The original homilies were written around the year 240. Unfortunately, the homilies are only preserved in a Latin version by Rufinus.

[7]For a text of the relevant section of Gregory's poem, see Metzger, *Canon*, p. 313. The list of New Testament books appears only in later manuscripts of the synod of Laodicea's decrees, and it may not go back to the council itself. Even if it does not, however, it was apparently thought to do so and surely reflects some widespread understanding of the extent of the canon. Metzger, *Canon*, p. 210. For the text, see Metzger, *Canon*, p. 312.

[8]Metzger, *Canon*, p. 217.

[9]For the texts, see Grant, *Second-Century Christianity*, pp. 105-106.

[10]Dionysius himself, however, did not dispute the canonicity of the Apocalypse.

[11]The translation is that of J. E. L. Oulton in the Loeb Classical Library edition.

[12]It is only fair to note, however, that Revelation had always been widely accepted in the West, unlike the East.

Chapter 3

Five Possible Ways to Interpret Biblical Prophecy

"Interpretation" is transferring meaning from one context to another, as, for example, from French to English. The goal of interpretation is to enable someone who does not understand the original context (e.g., French) to be able to grasp what is being said in the new one (e.g., English). Interpretation seeks to discover what the meaning of something was in the setting in which it first occurred and how that meaning can be rendered in another setting. Accordingly, a valid interpretation must do at least two things: First, it must discover a meaning that actually existed in the original context. Next, it must transfer that meaning accurately and clearly into the new one.

In the case of biblical prophecy translation involves a series of transfers. There is the transfer in language. A translator must take a text in ancient Hebrew, Aramaic, or Greek and render the meaning in a modern tongue. There is also a transfer involving literary symbolism. Biblical prophecy — especially, apocalyptic prophecy — uses a series of metaphors, including such things as beasts and horns, that had specific connotations when the prophecies first appeared, much as in modern political cartoons where animals stand for nations or political parties. A modern interpreter or exegete has the task of explaining what these ancient symbols meant or else of finding appropriate modern symbols that convey approximately the same message.

Of all the transfers, the most profound and troublesome in interpreting biblical prophecy is the transfer in chronological time. A biblical prophecy not only appeared in a particular time, but it also looked forward to another particular time. Thousands of years later we have to decide what that once future time is from our perspective. What was future from Jeremiah's day could be either future or past from our own, depending on our interpretation of what Jeremiah's message was.

In general it can be said there are at least five possible ways of interpreting a biblical prophecy depending on one's assumptions about the transfer in chronological time. We can assume that what was future from Jeremiah's perspective is also future from our own. In that case we must interpret the prophecy *futuristically*. Jeremiah was telling us about events to which we also can look forward. On the other hand, we can assume that what was future from Jeremiah's perspective must certainly be past from ours. Jeremiah was only interested in his own immediate future. Since we live more than two millennia after him, Jeremiah's immediate future is for us the distant past. Hence, we must interpret the prophecy *historically*. Jeremiah's prophecy only tells us about ancient history.

Another possibility is to assume that the transfer in chronological time cannot really be made. The link between a prophecy and its own time frame is indissoluble, and any attempt to impose a later chronological perspective is, therefore, doomed to fail. If a chronological transfer is an impossibility, then we must interpret a biblical prophecy in an exhortative, idealistic, or preterite way. According to an *exhortative* perspective a biblical prophecy is primarily an attempt to affect attitudes and actions, and so the validity of a prophecy is its ability to induce righteousness. The biblical prophet did not predict the future in order to provide information, but in order to get an audience to live more responsibly. The purpose of the prediction was to make the wicked repent and the virtuous remain steadfast. Sometimes the prophets' predictions were contingent. If the righteous would only remain steadfast, God would bless them. Moreover, even when prophecies were not contingent, the prophet knew that God was always free to change his mind and might in fact do so if the Israelites changed their ways. Because prophecies were primarily attempts to get people to change their attitudes and actions and sometimes were contingent, we should not evaluate a prophecy on the basis of its subsequent fulfillment. Indeed, we cannot even raise the question of whether contingent prophecies were fulfilled until we know how the hearers responded to the conditional threat or promise. Instead, the only appropriate means to determine a prophecy's worth is to determine its impact on behavior. The historical worth of a prophecy is whether it led to improved conduct in the past. The futuristic worth of a prophecy is whether it will lead to improved conduct in our own time or subsequently.

According to an *idealistic* perspective, a prophecy is only a specific application of a general principle, and today what we should concentrate on is the underlying principle. A biblical prophet was not primarily a clairvoyant who was making disinterested predictions based on arbitrary evidence. A biblical prophet was a theologian who was passionately concerned that God's will be done, and what the prophet predicted depended on whether the people were being faithful to God or not. If the people were worshipping God alone and were obeying his commandments, then the prophet predicted victory, prosperity, and health. If the people turned to other gods or oppressed the widow and the orphan and the stranger, then the prophet predicted defeat, economic disaster, or a plague. Two thousand years later the specific predictions are unimportant and often unclear. What is important are the underlying moral and theological ideals that the prophecy presupposed and undergirded.

Finally, we have the *preterite* approach. We can assume that a prophecy is a past statement that must simply be accepted as such and should not be updated. A prophecy like any historical fact has to be understood in terms of the circumstances that produced it. Subsequent events or the general applicability of underlying principles are irrelevant and misleading. The meaning of a prophecy is what it meant at the time it was first uttered. Later historical happenings and present-day needs contribute nothing to understanding the prophecy itself.

In general, each of these five interpretative approaches has its own strengths and limitations. The great strength of the futuristic approach is that it allows us to affirm the literal truth of prophecies that have not yet come to pass. From a futuristic perspective we need not doubt the accuracy of a biblical prediction that has as of yet not materialized. What was future for a biblical writer is future for us also. Hence, it can be claimed that none of God's word has failed. Consequently, the futuristic approach tends to be popular with biblical literalists and religious conservatives in general.

The futuristic approach, however, does not by any means solve all difficulties. To begin with, it cannot salvage *every* unfulfilled prophecy. Some biblical prophecies had time limits that have already expired, and the fulfillment of other prophecies is no longer conceivable. Thus, whatever we may do with Jesus' words, "There are some of those standing here who will by no means taste of death until they see the son of humanity coming in his kingdom" (Matt. 16:28), we cannot interpret them futuristically, since obviously everyone who was standing by Jesus at the time has long since died. Similarly, whatever we may do with Ezekiel's prediction of the restoration of the lost tribes under a Davidic king (Ezek. 37:15-28), we must admit that, now that those tribes have disappeared, a future fulfillment is out of the question.

An even more serious problem for a futuristic approach is that it cannot explain why God revealed what was to come so long before its fulfillment. Normally one assumes that God tells us what is most relevant to and helpful for our own lives. But a futuristic approach posits that God regularly revealed things that would not take place for at least thousands of years. Accordingly, these predictions were scarcely relevant to the people who first heard them or to those who for centuries passed on the tradition. Moreover, for all we know, biblical prophecies may not be relevant to us either. If God has already waited two or three thousand years, could he not wait two or three thousand more?

A final problem with a futuristic approach is that it raises the question of whether human beings are truly free. The futuristic school of interpretation presupposes that God has foreseen what is to come in some detail and so the future is already fixed. If the future is fixed, however, we can only wonder whether human beings are truly at liberty to make real choices. Down through the ages conservative theologians have labored to convince us that God's complete knowledge of coming events is fully compatible with human freedom. I confess that I am unconvinced.

Turning to the historical approach to biblical prophecy, we can see that it too has great strengths. The historical approach respects the fact that biblical prophets made specific predictions about coming events (e.g., the fall of Jerusalem). Unlike the futuristic approach, the historical one also acknowledges that biblical prophets were concerned about their short-term future, and, of course, this future is for us the distant past. It is natural to resort to a historical interpretation when what a prophet foretold actually came to pass. Thus, we normally interpret Amos's prediction of the fall of the Northern Kingdom or Jeremiah's of the fall of Jerusalem historically, since not too long after the prophecies the Northern Kingdom and Jerusalem did in fact fall. It also seems somehow more honest to admit that certain predictions (e.g., Ezekiel's prediction of the restoration of the lost tribes) simply did not come to pass rather than resort to a futuristic perspective.

Nevertheless, the historical approach has its problems, too. To begin with, as was just noted, historically certain prophecies simply did not occur. However, the fact that Jewish and Christian communities were able to remember even these prophecies and find edification in them strongly suggests that there must have been more in these texts than merely failed forecasts. In addition, historically not all biblical "prophecies" were predictions, and not all the predictions were sufficiently clear to enable us to determine whether there was a fulfillment or not. Thus, many of the "prophecies" in Daniel were not actually predictions, but were a recitation of events that were already past. The actual author of the book wrote around 165 B.C.E. However, he placed the book in the time of the Babylonian exile and had Daniel foresee what would subsequently occur. Similarly, it is difficult to interpret a prophecy like John 1:51 historically. The saying, "You shall see the heaven opened and the angels of God ascending and descending upon the son of humanity," is simply too cryptic for us even to attempt to determine whether historically it was fulfilled or not. Worst of all, the historical approach basically makes ancient prophecy irrelevant to us. If a prophecy concerns only what for us is the far past, then regardless of whether or not it was fulfilled, it is of no great consequence now.

The exhortative approach has two strong points. First, unlike the futuristic and historical approaches, the exhortative takes the goal of the biblical prophets seriously. The exhortative approach correctly insists that the goal of prophecy was not to give information but to improve conduct. Second, the exhortative approach allows us to salvage the truth of certain unfulfilled historical prophecies. If a prophecy led to a change in attitude and action, the prediction was true even if the forecast did not turn out to be accurate. We can see the great advantage of the exhortative approach by taking a look at the story of Jonah. In the story, Jonah predicts that Nineveh will be destroyed in forty days. When the inhabitants of the city hear the dreadful news, they repent utterly. As a result, God changes his mind and spares the city (Jonah 3). If we were to evaluate Jonah's prophecy using the historical approach we would have to say the forecast was false. God did not destroy the city after forty days. From an exhortative perspective, however, we can see the prophecy was completely true. God's purpose in sending Jonah was to get Nineveh to repent, and the threat to destroy the city was designed to achieve that purpose. Hence, the city's repentance vindicated the prophecy completely and made its literal fulfillment unnecessary.

Still, the exhortative approach has its difficulties. To begin with, most biblical prophecies — including those in Revelation — were not contingent. The prophets generally did not predict that God would do something unless the people repented, but simply that God would do something. Indeed, we have predictions that insist something will occur even if people change their behavior. Thus, at one point Amos predicts disaster and begs the people to repent. Still, the only hope that Amos holds for us is that perhaps *after* God has brought the disaster, he will then be gracious (Amos 5, especially, vs. 15). An even more serious difficulty with the exhortative approach is that we seldom know whether in response to a prophecy people actually lived differently. The Bible provides us with many, many prophecies, but only rarely records whether a prophecy led to improved conduct.

The great strength of the idealistic approach is that it makes biblical prophecy relevant, regardless of whether a prediction was fulfilled or not. As noted above, the idealistic approach sees biblical prophecies as specific applications of general principles. The biblical prophet started with certain basic convictions, such as God loves the poor and punishes those who oppress them. Then on the basis of these convictions the prophet made contingent predictions. Because these predictions are merely the expressions of something else, they are of relatively little importance themselves. Consequently, whether or not they were or will be fulfilled is of minor significance. What is important are the underlying principles. Since these are general, they tend to be as meaningful today as they were in ancient times. Consequently, preachers (often without realizing what they are doing) normally resort to idealistic exegesis. So it is that the classical prophets' concern for economic and political justice has had a great impact on modern theology, whereas the specific predictions based on this concern have not.

Nevertheless, the idealistic approach has its problems. First of all, there is something unsettling about dismissing so much as not important. Of course, biblical prophecies are contingent predictions based on general principles and so the underlying principles are important. However, to say the principles are important does not imply the predictions based on them are not equally significant. Clearly the specific application has its own integrity and should not be ignored. Indeed, the canonical prophets themselves often insisted that their message was superior because it, unlike the predictions of the "false prophets," would actually be fulfilled (see, for example, I Kings 22, especially vs. 28). In practice, another problem with the idealistic approach is that idealistic exegetes tend to focus only on those underlying principles with which they happen to be in agreement. Thus, as noted above, modern theologians have made much of the prophetic concern for the oppressed. However, they have ignored the prophetic theology that the God of Israel savagely punishes sinners and is capable of wiping out a city or even a whole people. A final problem with the idealistic approach is that it is not enough to identify the underlying principles. One must also explain why they are in fact valid. For example, is the principle that God punishes the ruthless valid because this principle normally generates correct predictions about the course of human affairs? Or is the principle valid only because it expresses how God feels about ruthlessness, namely that he abhors it?

Happily, the strengths and weaknesses of the preterite approach are evident and so do not require prolonged discussion. The great advantage of refusing to impose later perspectives on a prophecy is that the prophecy can then be understood in its own terms without distortion. Hence, the preterite approach is popular with historians, particularly "scientific" ones who strive to describe the past objectively. However, this great advantage is also a great disadvantage. If we refuse to impose later perspectives, we simply cannot focus on those questions and problems that are interesting to us. The prophecy becomes merely a relic of the past and ceases to have any relevance to our own situation. Not surprisingly, modern preterite commentaries on biblical material tend to be dry and frustrating to readers who want more than antiquarian information. It must also be added that the preterite approach conflicts with the biblical prophets' own self-understanding. From the prophets' viewpoint, subsequent perspectives were crucial to evaluating the original message because in the future God would validate the prophet's words by bringing them to pass.

Chapter 4

The Necessity and Difficulty of the Five Ways in Interpreting Revelation

In the last chapter we surveyed five approaches to interpreting a biblical prophecy and considered the strengths and weaknesses of each. Specifically, we saw that a prophecy can be interpreted futuristically, historically, or in an exhortative, idealistic, or preterite way and that each option both solves problems and creates them.

In the case of Revelation, each approach has been used. Thus, as we noted in the first chapter, many commentators down through the centuries have understood Revelation primarily futuristically. They have believed that the book portrays coming events. Valid exegesis of the apocalypse leads to sound forecasts concerning what will take place. One such modern commentator is Hal Lindsey, who deduces such things as the imminent rebuilding of the Jerusalem temple, the upcoming invasion of Palestine, and a nuclear war.[1]

By contrast, other commentators have understood Revelation primarily historically. They have held that at least much of the book predicted events that for us are now past. Indeed, it has been common to see in Revelation an outline of the history of the church from John's day to the consummation. A modern historical approach appears in the popular *Halley's Bible Handbook*. This handbook suggests that the first of Revelation's seven trumpets (Rev. 8:2-11:19) refers to the invasion of the Goths into Italy in the early fifth century; the second predicts the subsequent invasion of the Vandals; the third foretells the attacks of Attila the Hun; the fourth "Odeacer's seizure of Rome;"[2] and the fifth trumpet tells of "the rise and spread of Mohammedanism."[3]

Still other commentators have interpreted the Apocalypse in an exhortative way. They see Revelation primarily as an attempt to change the behavior of the churches to which John wrote, and they use texts from Revelation in order to challenge our behavior today. It is especially logical to use an exhortative approach when one deals with the seven letters in Revelation 2-3, since these directly exhort the various churches.

Terence Kelshaw provides an illustration of the exhortative approach in his book *Send This Message to My Church.*[4]   Kelshaw sees the seven letters in Revelation 2-3 as addressing basic problems in the churches of Asia Minor and providing Christian solutions. He contends that similar problems still exist in congregations today. Accordingly, "this biblical mail is also addressed to *us*." He notes that a recurring theme in the letters is the need not to compromise our faith by assimilating Christianity to popular culture and that the temptation to debase our faith in order to be socially acceptable is rife now. Hence, "God is *still* issuing in these letters a warning against such apostasy."[5]

Still other commentators have interpreted the book idealistically, by focusing on theological and moral principles. As nearly as I can tell, this approach is not as popular today as it has been in certain times and places in the past (e.g., in the allegorizing school of ancient Alexandria). Nevertheless, even today, occasionally works appear that focus almost exclusively on the general theological ideas which underlie John's more specific prophecies.   Thus, Jacques Ellul's book on the Apocalypse assures us that for John "the circumstantial is only the occasion to denote a more profound, universal, and fundamental reality." Ellul proceeds to claim, for example, that the first beast in Revelation 13 is not so much the Roman Empire as "political power in the global, universal sense."[6]

Finally, most modern mainline scholars have interpreted the book in a preterite way. Here R. H. Charles' two-volume classic sets the tone for subsequent work.[7]   Today most scholars who are not committed to upholding a tradition of denominational exegesis view the apocalypse as a product of John's own day that addresses the needs of that time.

In my opinion, there is no escaping the fact that each of these approaches is both necessary and yet problematic for the interpretation of the Apocalypse. The futuristic approach is essential if Revelation as a whole is to be judged a success. The climax of the Apocalypse, namely the appearance of a new heaven and earth and the descent of the New Jerusalem, clearly has not yet occurred. If these climactic events are *in no sense* still to come, then the work basically fails. At most, certain parts of Revelation may be helpful, but the book taken as a whole is false.

The futuristic approach also suffers from severe difficulties. To begin with, as we have noted already, futuristic predictions based on Revelation have so far always proved to be at least premature. After nearly two millennia of failed predictions we can only wonder how much longer we should persevere going down a road that has so long led to a dead end. In addition, Revelation insists that its predictions will all be fulfilled "soon" (Rev. 1:1, 1:3, etc.), and in this context "soon" cannot mean in two thousand years. Revelation addresses seven historical first-century churches, and it is to *them* that the book promises speedy relief. Hence, "soon" must be soon enough to be comforting to a Christian living when the writing first appeared. Of course, from that perspective "soon" is not two millennia. No one would be greatly relieved by the assurance that speedy help was on the way and would (in just two thousand years!) actually arrive.

The historical approach is essential if Revelation is to be judged a success in order to deal with the book's insistence that its promises would be fulfilled "soon." Since "soon" cannot be two thousand years, then if Revelation's predictions were valid, *something must already have happened* that delivered John's original readers from their tribulation. Moreover, it cannot be argued that "soon" is a minor theme in Revelation and, therefore, its lack of fulfillment relatively unimportant. On the contrary, the promise of speedy help appears throughout the book (e.g., Rev. 3:11) and receives emphasis both in the work's introduction (Rev. 1:1, 1:3) and conclusion (Rev. 22:20).

However, there are severe problems with the historical approach. To begin with, Revelation clearly understands "soon" to be "soon" to the consummation, and the consummation has not occurred. In addition, Revelation's predictions are mostly so bizarre and so vague that it is hard to correlate them convincingly with historic persons and events; attempts to do so have failed. Thus, despite the richness of Revelation's description of the demonic locusts, we can scarcely identify them with anything we have seen in history so far. What have we witnessed that looked like horses with golden crowns, human faces, women's hair, lion's teeth, and iron breastplates (to give but part of the description)? To make an identification we must selectively ignore some of these features, and such selectivity in the end makes the identification wholly subjective. Thus, Halley's *Bible Handbook* identifies the locusts with the Islamic horsemen who conquered much of Christendom in the seventh and eighth centuries. In justification we read, "This [Rev. 9:7-10] is indeed a very good description of Mohammedan armies, composed of fierce, relentless horsemen, famous for their beards, with long hair like women's hair, with yellow turbans on their heads that looked like gold, and they had iron coats of armor."[8] Yet, despite the ingenuity, this identification is clearly wrong. We receive no explanation of such features as the lion's teeth. Even more important, in Revelation the locusts only harm those "who do not have the seal of God upon their foreheads" (Rev. 9:4), whereas the Islamic invaders were a scourge to *Christians*.

Likewise the exhortative approach is needed and yet problematic. The exhortative approach is needed because John's primary goal in writing Revelation was to change the behavior of his readers and, therefore, the success of the prophecy must, at least in part, be judged on whether the book has had the desired impact on conduct. Unfortunately, however, it is not clear that Revelation's impact on behavior has been positive. We really have no way to assess how the book affected the churches to which John wrote. No minutes have come down to us from the gatherings at which the Apocalypse was first read. We know a great deal more about Revelation's impact on subsequent generations, but often that impact is difficult to view positively. Revelation generally had the most visible effect on the attitudes and actions of people who believed that the world was about to end. However, whether in light of subsequent events we should view that effect as positive is problematic to say the least.

The idealistic approach to interpreting Revelation is also indispensable, but it too has its difficulties. Since there has been no clear fulfillment of Revelation's prophecies and at this late date a fulfillment now appears hardly likely, it seems only logical to try to get something edifying out of Revelation by looking for the enduring principles that inspired the book. Moreover, the fact that the church has been able to make use of Revelation for nearly two thousand years strongly suggests that Revelation must indeed contain such principles. In addition, it is striking that Revelation itself often seems to interpret the prophecies of the Old Testament idealistically. When the Apocalypse takes over images and language from Old Testament prophetic and apocalyptic writings, Revelation tends to synthesize and generalize. Thus, the description of the Great City and its fate (Rev. 17:1-19:4) draws heavily on Old Testament polemic against various cities, including Babylon and Tyre (compare, for example, Ezekiel 26-27 and Jeremiah 50-51 with Revelation 18:1-24); the description of the Beast from the Sea (Rev. 13:1-10) takes elements from each of the four beasts in Daniel 7:1-8. This tendency to borrow, synthesize, and generalize suggests John felt that such things as the forces of evil and what happens to them are always the same. In other words, it appears that John saw a set of timeless principles in earlier prophetic texts, and it was these principles that especially interested him. Moreover, at times the specific principles John discovered and used are clearly visible. For example, in biblical thought the punishment, ideally, is similar to the crime (Wisdom of Solomon 11:16). The wicked dig a pit for the righteous and fall into it themselves (e.g., Ps. 7:14-16), or the Egyptians worship animals and God punishes them by the various animals (e.g., frogs) of the ten plagues (e.g., Wisdom of Solomon 15:18-16:1). We see a clear example of this principle in Revelation 16:4-6. When the third angel pours out his bowl and the rivers become blood, he says to God, "You are righteous . . . because they shed the blood of saints and prophets, and you have given to them blood to drink." Nevertheless, the idealistic approach does not solve all our problems. For better or worse, Revelation remains a specific prophecy, and no amount of attention to underlying principles will change what the book basically is.

Finally, in interpreting Revelation the preterite approach is essential, since it is the method with which we must begin, even if it does not take us as far as we need to go. We must begin with the preterite approach because we can only legitimately ask what Revelation means now after we have discovered what it first meant when it was written. Interpreters can only transfer the meaning of a text from one context to another after they find out what the meaning in the initial context was. An interpretation that does not proceed from the original meaning has no real foundation and is always in danger of being wholly arbitrary. Moreover, from the perspective of Christian theology the doctrine of the incarnation seems to point to the preterite approach as the proper place to start. The incarnation implies that God came to us in a unique situation and that, therefore, God must first be known as he revealed himself in a particular context before he can be known in general. Hence, before we can discover what the general message of the Apocalypse is to all times and places (or to our time and place) we must first discover what its message was to its own time and place. A final strength of the preterite approach is that it sometimes gives convincing solutions to specific problems that neither the futuristic nor the historical approaches can solve. Thus, as we noted, scholars who have interpreted Revelation's prophecies historically have produced many conflicting explanations for the number "666" and the identity of the Beast. From a preterite perspective, however, the identity of the Beast is clear. It is the emperor Nero. Nero was the first emperor to persecute Christians, and, after he died, there were persistent rumors that he was alive and would return to culminate his destructive activities. The beast in Revelation fits this description exactly, since in Revelation 17:10-11 we learn that the Beast is both one of five past rulers and yet is still to come. Nero's name even adds up to the necessary number. For the Jewish Christian author of Revelation the sacred language would have been Hebrew, even though he was writing in Greek.[9] If we take the Greek name "Neron Caesar" and transliterate it into Hebrew, the resulting letters add up to 666.[10] Despite all the insight the preterite method can give us, however, it can only be the method with which we start—not the one with which we end. By itself the preterite approach merely tells us what Revelation meant when it was first written, and so, if we stick solely to this method, we cannot even ask the question of what Revelation means now. Of course, if we do not go on to this question, Revelation simply is irrelevant to our concerns. Nevertheless, the preterite approach remains the one with which we must begin.

Notes

[1]Hal Lindsey with C. C. Carlson, *The Late Great Planet Earth* (Grand Rapids: Zondervan, 1970), pp. 152-166.

[2]Henry H. Halley, *Bible Handbook: An Abbreviated Bible Commentary* (Chicago: the author, 20th ed., 1955), p. 635.

[3]Halley, *Bible Handbook*, p. 636.

[4]Terence Kelshaw, *Send This Message to My Church: Christ's Words to the Seven Churches of Revelation* (Nashville: Thomas Nelson, 1984).

[5]Kelshaw, *Send This Message*, p. 21. Emphasis in the original.

[6]Jacques Ellul, *Apocalypse: The Book of Revelation* (New York: Seabury, 1977), p. 92.

[7]R. H. Charles, *A Critical and Exegetical Commentary on the Revelation of St. John* (New York: Scribner's, 1920).

[8]Halley, *Bible Handbook*, p. 637.

[9]It is noteworthy that Rev. 9:11 gives to the "Angel of the Abyss" a Hebrew name which John then translates for his readers.

[10]Using Nero as the solution we can also explain a divergent reading. A few ancient copies of Revelation read not "666" but "616." If we pronounce "Nero" in the Latin way rather than the Greek, (i.e., omitting the final "n") and transliterate that into Hebrew, we get "616."

PART II

Revelation's Historical Background
and Literary Structure
and Original Message

Chapter 5

Revelation's Old Testament and Intertestamental Background and Its Significance

Even though it does not actually quote the Old Testament, Revelation draws heavily on it. Unlike such New Testament writers as Matthew and Paul, John does not cite scripture verbatim. Nevertheless, he has many allusions to it. Swete's classic commentary lists around two hundred.[1] Other scholarly works have claimed even more.[2]

Revelation relies perhaps most on Daniel. Much of John's imagery comes from there. Swete notes, "In proportion to its length the Book of Daniel yields by far the greatest number" of allusions.[3] Paulien calculates that only the short books of Zechariah and Joel have a higher proportion of their contents present in Revelation.[4] A great deal of John's theology also seems to come from Daniel. Thus, Daniel proclaims that in the endtime an evil ruler will institute a catastrophic persecution of God's people. Shortly thereafter, God will intervene by destroying the ruler and his empire. Then he will raise the dead and punish the wicked and reward the righteous. Revelation, of course, proclaims the same.

Revelation also has important similarities to ancient Jewish visionary works such as I & II Enoch and II Esdras. Thus, I Enoch tells us that Enoch journeyed to heaven and beheld the splendor of God's throne room (I Enoch 14:6-25) and provides us with a long prophecy in which animals represent historical characters (I Enoch 85-90). Similarly, Revelation tells us that John ascended to heaven and saw the splendor of God's throne room (Rev. 4) and uses animal symbolism to foretell future events (Rev. 13 and 17). Because of such parallels scholars have traditionally labelled documents like Daniel and I Enoch "apocalypses."[5]

Theologically, such visionary works as Daniel and I Enoch made a permanent contribution to Christian thought. In these we encounter important ideas that have ever after been foundations of church belief. Indeed, these ideas are so central that it is easy to forget that they are rare in Old Testament thought prior to apocalyptic and that for centuries Israelite religion apparently did without them.

One great contribution to subsequent orthodoxy was the discovery of eternal life. Previously, the Jews had believed that meaningful life ended at death. After death the spirit went to Sheol, a shadowy realm where the deceased's consciousness decayed along with the flesh. Only with Daniel and such works as I Enoch do we have a clear and self-conscious affirmation that humans have an eternal life with God following one's physical demise. Thus, Daniel provides us with the sole Old Testament text that undeniably affirms resurrection from the dead (Dan. 12:2)[6], and I Enoch gives us passages that describe the bliss of the saved and the misery of the damned (e.g., I Enoch 22). Significantly, the Sadducees who rejected writings like Daniel and I Enoch denied that there is meaningful existence after death.

Another major contribution to subsequent thought was the conscious realization that history has a transcendent goal. Prior to the apocalypses biblical authors mostly assumed either that history is cyclic and so merely repeats itself or that God has an everlasting earthly covenant with Israel that assures the nation of special privileges in this order of existence. In neither case was human history looked at as a whole and seen as a preparation for some greater consummation—a consummation exceeding anything we can experience in this world. Such works as Daniel and II Esdras, however, attempt to look at all of history and see it as a preparation for some greater blessedness beyond what is possible now. Thus, Daniel 2:31-45 divides history into four ages of decreasing perfection and affirms that at the end of this devolution God will suddenly intervene and usher in a new age that will last forever. II Esdras 7 looks forward to a four-hundred-year messianic reign and a subsequent general resurrection and final judgment of the nations (II Esdras 7:28-44).

If in some respects the apocalypses advanced theology, they also have features that seem dubious, especially today. To begin with, the apocalypses resort to pseudonymity. Literally, pseudonymity means "false name." The works claim to be by ancient worthies even though the actual authors lived much later. Thus, a great deal of Daniel (chs. 7-12) claims to be a firsthand report from a hero who flourished during the Babylonian exile. The real writer, however, composed the book in the second century B.C.E. To us pseudonymity seems like forgery. No doubt, pseudonymity was more acceptable in ancient times since it was widely practiced.   Nevertheless, we must assume that even then there was something illegitimate about gratuitously claiming the authority of a revered figure from the past.   John Barton's comments seem judicious. "There can have been little point in pseudepigraphy unless one's probable readers could understand a claim to authorship and thought that it mattered who the author of a book was."   "Authors of pseudonymous works, then, were making a claim that was capable of being true or false, and it was in fact false."[7]   Pseudonymity seems especially dubious when it generates retrospective "prophecy."   In Daniel, I Enoch, and a number of other apocalypses, the purported author foresees the events of subsequent history. Of course, from the perspective of the actual author most of these events were already past and so no insight was required to "predict" them.

To us a second questionable feature of the apocalypses is they reveal esoteric mysteries that from our perspective the authors could scarcely have known.   The apocalypses tell us about the orbits of heavenly bodies, the events of the primordial past, the geography of distant places.[8] The books claim this knowledge came through visions. Today we would doubt whether visions provide us with detailed information concerning such disciplines as astronomy, ancient history, and geography.

If we now turn to Revelation, we can see it retains the advances of the "apocalypses." Revelation affirms the resurrection of the dead and eternal life (e.g., Rev. 20:11ff.). It emphasizes that the life to come is qualitatively superior to anything we can experience in this age and so provides a fitting consummation to human history.   In the New Jerusalem we can eat of the tree of life that Adam and Eve lost in the beginning (Rev. 22:2).

Revelation does not, however, perpetuate the defects of apocalyptic. Thus, Revelation is not pseudonymous. John explicitly writes under his own name (Rev. 1:1, 1:4, etc.) and even describes himself as the readers' brother and partner (Rev. 1:9). Consequently, Revelation contains no recitation of past events as if they were future. Quite the contrary, Revelation explicitly talks about the present as present. The author writes not only about what is to be but even about what already is (Rev. 1:19), and in the letters to the churches John directly discusses contemporary issues in ecclesiastical life (Rev. 2-3).

In addition, unlike I Enoch and many apocalypses, Revelation does not provide us with a lot of impressive esoteric information. Revelation does not tell us about the forgotten events of primordial history or the hidden structure of the heavens. As Rowland puts it, Revelation does not reveal things that merely satisfy our "curiosity."[9]

Because of these differences in content, Revelation seems more honest to us. John does not try to pass off his own work as the product of a great saint of old. He does not claim to be revealing mysteries that from our perspective no one could possibly know. Instead, he takes responsibility for his own visions and sticks to matters for which he himself can vouch and that are relevant to his audience's immediate concerns.

In his own day, this honesty raised questions concerning the book's credibility. By resorting to pseudonymity, the authors of other "apocalypses" endowed their works with the authority of some revered figure of the past. By revealing what no one could know on their own, the other apocalypses made their claims to divine inspiration incontestable. Hence, in dropping these devices, John invited the question of whether his own message was credible. This question was especially likely to arise because, as we shall see, he was asking his readers to bet their lives on the truth of his predictions. Significantly, within the visions, characters assure John that what he is learning is "trustworthy and true" (Rev. 21:5, 22:6; cf. 19:9).

One way John responded to the issue of credibility was to claim that he was a prophet. Like other early Christians, John believed the Holy Spirit that had departed from Israel was now present in the church (cf., e.g., Acts. 2:1-21) and had renewed the gift of prophecy. John claims that the Spirit has inspired his own work. He specifically calls his book a "prophecy" (Rev. 1:3, 22:18-19). Like the classical prophets he narrates a scene in which he receives God's word and the command to share it (Rev. 10:8-11; cf. 1:1-2). Significantly, the scene closely parallels Ezekiel's call (Ezek. 2:8-3:3).

The statement that one is a prophet need not be true, however, and so later we will consider whether John's claim is justified (see below chapters 9-16). John himself denounces an influential seer in the church at Thyatira who "calls herself a prophetess" (Rev. 2:20). According to him, she is a new "Jezebel" who leads God's people astray (Rev. 2:20). Hence, we will have to scrutinize the spiritual basis of John's own prophetic utterances and determine whether they are in fact true.

Notes

[1]Henry Barclay Swete, *The Apocalypse of St. John* (London: MacMillan, 1907), pp. cxxxix-xliii. Swete states that his table is "not exhaustive."

[2]With some exaggeration, Milligan writes: "It may be doubted whether it [Revelation] contains a single figure not drawn from the Old Testament, or a single complete sentence not more or less built up of materials brought from the same source." Quoted in Jon Paulien, *Decoding Revelation's Trumpets: Literary Allusions and Interpretations of Revelation 8:7-12* (Berrien Springs: Andrew's University Press, 1988), p. 14.

[3]Swete, *Apocalypse*, p. cliii.

[4]Paulien, *Decoding*, pp. 46-47, note 4.

[5]Here we need not enter into the scholarly debate over how to define an "apocalypse" and which books meet the definition. Whatever conclusions we may come to today, we cannot assume John would have agreed. For an important modern attempt to define and classify apocalypses, see John L. Collins, ed., *Apocalypse: The Morphology of a Genre, Semeia* 14 (1979).

[6]The only other likely references are Isaiah 25:8; 26:19.

[7]John Barton, *Oracles of God: Perceptions of Ancient Prophecy in Israel After the Exile* (London: Darton, Longman and Todd, 1986), p. 211.

[8]For a detailed review of the esoteric knowledge the apocalypses reveal, see Christopher Rowland, *The Open Heaven: A Study of Apocalyptic in Judaism and Early Christianity* (New York: Crossroad, 1982), especially pp. 73-189.

[9]Rowland, *Open Heaven*, p. 415.

Chapter 6

Revelation's Social Setting

Revelation provides us with a fair amount of material which we can use to reconstruct John's understanding of what was going on when he wrote. Revelation contains seven short letters to different congregations, and these letters seem to reflect concrete situations in the specific communities in question (Rev. chapters 2-3). The letters deal with different problems in each church and sometimes even mention local groups and individuals by name, though to be sure, the names are generally also symbolic. For example, in the letter to the church of Ephesus we read of "those who call themselves apostles" (Rev. 2:2) and the "Nicolaitans" (Rev. 2:6), and in the letter to the church of Smyrna we read of those "who say they are Jews and are not" (Rev. 2:9). The letters also appear to fit the larger urban communities in which the churches were located. The letter to Laodicea is especially apt for its geographical setting. The epistle complains that the congregation claims to be rich when in fact it is "poor and blind and naked" (Rev. 3:17). The author then counsels this church to buy pure gold and white garments and to anoint their eyes with salve (Rev. 3:18). It is striking that in the first century Laodicea was notoriously wealthy and a center for the manufacture of clothing and eye ointment but that the clothing in question was mostly made of *black* wool.[1]

If the letters to the seven churches give us details about the special circumstances of particular congregations, chapters 13 and 17 present the author's understanding of the larger political situation he feared would soon influence the church. To be sure, as elsewhere, John uses symbols. However, here there can be no question that the basic figures represent social and political forces, and we can be tolerably certain what the specific references are. Thus, in chapter 13 the Beast from the Sea undoubtedly stands for the Roman government, and the heads of the Beast represent individual emperors. Similarly, the Whore in chapter 17 who is named "Babylon the Great" (Rev. 17:5) and sits on seven hills

(Rev. 17:9) and rules over the kings of the earth (Rev. 17:18) can only be the city of Rome.

From the seven letters we learn that Revelation addresses Christian communities in Western Asia Minor (modern Turkey). The seven cities that the letters explicitly address are all located in this region. It seems likely, however, that John actually addresses all the Christian communities in the area. Throughout Revelation the number "7" is used symbolically and represents totality. Hence, "the seven churches in Asia" (Rev. 1:4) probably means all the churches in Asia. Significantly, the different letters portray different basic situations and, taken together, they almost exhaust the possible circumstances of a congregation. Thus, we hear both of a church that has forsaken its "first love" (Rev. 2:4) and a church whose last works exceed the first (Rev. 2:19), of a church that excludes heretics (Rev. 2:2, 6) and one that tolerates them (Rev. 2:14-15), of a church that is spiritually rich and materially poor (Rev. 2:9) and one that is materially rich but spiritually poor (Rev. 3:17). Accordingly, the letters of Revelation would have had something to say to almost any conceivable Christian group in ancient Asia Minor. It is noteworthy that toward the end of each letter John says, "Hear what the spirit is saying to the church*es*" (plural!). Of course, the letters retain their universality today.

From the data Revelation gives us we can see that John is concerned about several things. Jewish Christianity is under great pressure from non-Christian Jews, and the churches are failing. The letters to Smyrna and Philadelphia clearly suggest that these congregations were primarily Jewish. John finds nothing to criticize about these two congregations themselves since they are not engaging in such Gentile Christian failings as eating meat sacrificed to idols (cf. Rev. 2:14, 2:20). However, humanly speaking, the churches are in trouble. The church in Smyrna is experiencing "affliction and poverty" (Rev. 2:9), and the church in Philadelphia has "little power" (Rev. 3:8). This situation seems to be due to the opposition of people who "say they are Jews and are not" (Rev. 2:9, 3:9) whom John labels a "synagogue of Satan" (Rev. 2:9, 3:9). Apparently, the synagogues were gaining control over the Jewish community as a whole, and, consequently, Jewish Christianity was withering. Revelation also suggests that Gentile Christianity was increasingly making concessions to paganism. Humanly speaking, Gentile Christianity appeared to be prospering. Indeed, the church in Laodicea was in a position to boast, "I have become rich and have no need of anything" (Rev. 3:17). However, John insists that, spiritually speaking, these congregations are in trouble. Thus, all the seven letters except those to Smyrna and Philadelphia criticize the respective churches and threaten them with final rejection unless they repent. John censures them for their willingness to compromise with pagan practice. These congregations allow eating meat which was sacrificed to idols (Rev. 2:14, 2:20). Perhaps they also permit members to engage in certain forms of pagan worship, since John complains that at Thyatira "Jezebel" teaches people to commit "fornication" (Rev. 2:20). Here "fornication" probably refers to worshipping other gods (including the Roman emperor), since that is what "fornication" normally refers to in Revelation and in much of the Old Testament. John also foresees a supreme crisis. Soon the Roman emperor will insist that everyone worship him and decree that anyone who refuses be put to death. As a result, faithful Christians will be slaughtered. In chapter 13 we have a nightmarish scene in which everyone must worship the image of the Beast from the Sea or perish and, as a result, the saints are destroyed (Rev. 13:5-18).

From the information recorded in chapter 17 it might seem that we should be able to determine who the emperor was when Revelation was written, but unfortunately we cannot. At first glance it appears that what Revelation tells us about the heads of the Beast reveals who the reigning ruler was. Verses 17:9-10 say that the seven heads of the Beast are seven kings and that the sixth is presently in power. Regrettably, however, it is difficult to figure out who John's sixth emperor was. We do not know whether John thought the first Roman emperor was Julius Caesar who was the first person who assumed this title or Augustus who was the first of the continuous line of emperors. We also do not know whether John counted the three emperors who reigned very briefly during the unsettled period from July 69 to July 70. Finally, we do not know whether John somehow fudged in order to make the line of emperors correspond to his numerology. As we shall later see in more detail (see the appendix to chapter 7 below), the numbers "six" and "seven" have special meaning for John. "Six" is the number he associates with evil and "seven" the number he associates with completion. Hence, if John regarded the reigning emperor as an enemy of the church, he would have wanted to make him the sixth king. Similarly, since John regards "seven" as the number of completion, it would be natural for him to make the last emperor in his series the seventh. John's numbering of the imperial line fits his numerology, and so we must wonder whether John adopted some special system of enumeration to make the figures come out right. Perhaps, for example, John began his list of emperors not with Julius Caesar or Augustus but with the first ruler he believed was significant for the Christian church.

Despite our uncertainty regarding John's numbering, it is probable that Revelation was written toward the end of the first century and, more specifically, during the last years of Domitian's reign (81-96). Revelation could not have been written much earlier. Revelation's references to Roman politics clearly presuppose the end of Nero's reign in the year 68 and the crushing of the Jewish Revolt in 70. The eighth king who is one of the seven (Rev. 17:11) can only be Nero returning after his death. Similarly, "Babylon" would only be an appropriate symbol for Rome after Rome, like Babylon of old, had destroyed Jerusalem and the temple. The information that Revelation gives about the histories of the seven churches strongly suggests a date after 80 or so. The congregation of Ephesus that Paul helped begin (cf. I Cor. 16:8-9) has now abandoned its "first love" (Rev. 2:4). According to its second-century bishop Polycarp, the church of Smyrna did not exist during Paul's time (Polycarp to the Philippians 11). According to the Alogoi, the church at Thyatira did not exist during the life of John the Apostle (Epiphanius, *Haer.* 51.33.1). Yet Revelation assumes that both congregations are firmly established and even tells us that Thyatira's "last works are more than the first" (Rev. 2:19). By contrast, there is less proof that Revelation could not have been written sometime after Domitian's reign. In my opinion, the decisive piece of evidence that Revelation came from the final years of Domitian's rule is the explicit testimony of Irenaeus, who writes that the apocalypse was "almost in our own time, at the end of the reign of Domitian" (Eusebius, *Eccles. Hist.* 3.18.1-3). This testimony is probably reliable because Irenaeus was a student of Polycarp who lived in Asia Minor during Domitian's reign.

It would be extremely helpful for us as we try to evaluate Revelation to know if Domitian forced people to worship himself and persecuted Christians. As we have seen, Revelation predicts that there will be a catastrophic imperial persecution. Was this prediction based on what the emperor was actually beginning to do when John wrote? We would like to know whether John discerned the signs of the times and drew conclusions from them or instead based his forecast only on dogmatic or biblical considerations.

Unfortunately, it is difficult to determine what Domitian's policy toward emperor worship and Christians was. On the one hand, we have good ancient sources that report the emperor insisted he be worshipped and he fiercely persecuted the church. The historian Suetonius, who lived through Domitian's reign, portrays him as a megalomaniac who insisted on being addressed as "Lord and God" (Suetonius, *Dom.* 8.13.2). The fourth-century historian Eusebius states that Domitian was second only to Nero in his ferocity toward the church (*Eccles. Hist.* 3.17-20). Yet on the other hand, serious questions arise concerning the accuracy of these statements. The title "Lord and God" is usually absent from documents that Domitian's supporters wrote in praise of him.[2] Similarly, the only specific illustrations of persecution that Eusebius gives are the banishing of Domitilla, the interrogation of the descendants of Jude, and the exiling of John (the author of Revelation). Surely, if there had been a serious persecution, Eusebius would have provided us with accounts of martyrdoms. Accordingly, it is not surprising that at least one modern scholar has argued that Domitian's religious policies were in no way oppressive.[3]

My own opinion is that the disturbing conditions of Domitian's last years put increasing pressure on people to worship the emperor and that many Christians, including those in Asia Minor, were subject to this pressure. In his last years Domitian executed more and more people on various charges involving disloyalty. Some of these charges were undoubtedly well founded. In the year 88 Saturninus the legate in upper Germany declared himself emperor and led an unsuccessful revolt. Moreover, in the end Domitian was actually assassinated in a palace conspiracy. However, the very real dangers that surrounded Domitian also inspired exaggerated suspicions. Under such circumstances it is likely that there was increasing pressure to worship the emperor or at least his deified father and brother. Worshipping the emperors was a tangible demonstration of loyalty, and to refuse to engage in it was to court disaster. We must suppose that the pressure to worship Domitian and his deceased relatives was at least as great in John's Asia Minor as elsewhere. The cult of the emperor was well established in the cities to which John wrote. Indeed, a temple to Domitian and his deified relatives was dedicated at Ephesus in the year 89/90, the approximate period in which John wrote.[4] The officials in Asia Minor had every reason to do all they could to allay the emperor's suspicions since Domitian executed the Asian proconsul for plotting against him (Suetonius, *Dom.* 8.10.2).

Even in normal times everyone was expected to take part in the honoring of the emperors, and in these extraordinary times officials would have labored to ensure that in fact everyone did take part. Hence, the pressure on Christians must have been considerable.

From John's perspective the situation of the Christian communities in Asia Minor was a matter of urgent concern. The overall content of Revelation makes it clear that John's theology was Jewish and conservative. It is noteworthy, for example, that he explicitly forbids eating meat sacrificed to idols (Rev. 2:14, 20), whereas Paul basically allowed it (I Cor. 10:23-33). From a conservative Jewish Christian vantage point the present circumstances were dire and the anticipated ones worse. When John was writing, conservative Jewish Christianity, as found at Smyrna and Philadelphia was failing, and the rest of the church was increasingly compromising with paganism. The most catastrophic imaginable crisis was also at hand – compulsive universal emperor worship. If we may judge from the tone of the seven letters, the churches were mostly unprepared.

It is probably not going too far to say that John felt personally responsible for the welfare of the congregations. He writes as someone who is well known to the reader and whose authority is recognized. Certainly, he is acquainted with each church's specific situation. Accordingly, one assumes he had visited at least some of the congregations and that he would be visiting them now if he were not on Patmos. Eusebius is probably correct when he tells us that John was in exile there (*Eccles. Hist.* 3.18.1).

The writing and sending of Revelation was his personal response to the crisis. Since John could not come, he sent the book, and it is noteworthy that the document is basically in the form of a letter (especially, Rev. 1:4). Revelation was John's personal pastoral admonition to his congregations in the face of their present and imminent difficulties.

Appendix I: The Structure and Order of the Seven Letters

The structure of the seven letters is very tight. Each letter begins with the phrase "to the angel of the church in _____ write." Then we have, "I know" followed by an attribute of Christ taken from the descriptions of him in chapter 1. The body of the letters follows and consists of praise or blame and admonitions. Toward the end of the admonitions Jesus assures us he is coming. Finally, we have the sentence, "Let those who have ears hear what the Spirit is saying to the churches" and the eschatological promise, "To the one who conquers . . ." In the earlier letters the promise comes last, whereas in the later ones it comes first.

The order of the letters is interesting on two counts. First it is a possible order in which one could visit the seven communities. Geographically, the cities lie in a rough circle. One could begin at Ephesus and go north to Smyrna and Pergamum then southeast to Thyatira, Sardis, and Philadelphia and southwest to Laodicea. Perhaps John intended for Revelation to be a circular letter and for one congregation to send it on to the next in the sequence he gives. John's order also produces alternating praise and blame. The letter to Ephesus is perhaps the most balanced with the praise and blame being about equal. Subsequently, positive and negative letters alternate. Thus, the epistle to Smyrna is wholly complimentary, the one to Pergamum more negative than positive, and the one to Thyatira more positive than negative. Then the epistle to Sardis is almost wholly negative, the one to Philadelphia wholly positive, and the one to Laodicea wholly negative. This order, of course, causes the praise and blame to stand out and so increases the pastoral impact of the letters.

Appendix II: Emperor Worship

From a pagan perspective emperor worship was a mandatory gesture of patriotism. Worshipping the emperor was a tangible sign of loyalty to the government and was expected of everyone except the Jews. Consequently, such worship was a basic component of civic social life. Indeed, in Asia Minor, there were special festivals that involved a whole city. The festivals might include parades and athletic contests as well as strictly cultic activities like sacrifices to or for the imperial family.

Accordingly, in many ways, the worship of the emperor in ancient Asia Minor did not differ all that much from the honoring of the royal family in modern England. Today, too, honoring the reigning monarch is a tangible gesture of loyalty and is expected of normal citizens. It is also (at least theoretically) the justification for parades and sporting activities.

Of course, like all worship that of the emperor tended to instill uncritical awe and obedience. Psychologically, adoration is incompatible with criticism. We cannot wholeheartedly reverence someone as divine and at the same time be aware of their human failings.

Because of their monotheism Christians refused to worship the emperor, and this refusal was one reason the early Christians were persecuted. Christianity inherited from Judaism the belief that there is only one God and the insistence that worship can be given to no one else. In practice the Roman government excused Jews from worshipping the emperor, since the Jews were an ethnic community and their custom of refusing to worship rulers was ancient. Once the Romans discovered that Christians were not traditional Jews, the Romans insisted that Christians must worship the gods, including the emperor. Because Christians refused, a series of persecutions ensued until the fourth century.

From the perspective of long-term history the refusal to worship the emperor contributed to the rise of democracy and a greater respect for human rights. In areas where Christianity became the predominant religion, rulers acknowledged they were only human beings. This acknowledgement tended to make them more accountable to their subjects. Especially in Western Europe church leaders felt free to criticize the government for injustice. It is no accident that democracy and constitutional guarantees of human rights primarily arose in Christian Europe and from there spread to the rest of the world.

Notes

[1]For a thorough discussion of the local allusions in the seven letters, see Colin J. Hemer, *The Letters to the Seven Churches of Asia in Their Local Setting* (Sheffield: JSOT Press, 1986).

[2]See Leonard L. Thompson, *The Book of Revelation: Apocalypse and Empire* (Oxford: Oxford University Press, 1990), pp. 105-106. There can, however, be no doubt that at least occasionally people called Domitian by this title since, as Thompson notes, Martial did.

[3]Thompson, *Apocalypse and Empire*, especially pp. 104-107.

[4]Price believes this dedication was the specific occasion which prompted John to write. See S. R. F. Price, *Rituals and Power: The Roman Imperial Cult in Asia Minor* (Cambridge: Cambridge University Press, 1984), pp. 197-198. I also have consulted the summary of Steven John Friesen's Ph.D. dissertation, "Ephesus, Twice Neokoros," the summary of which is in *Harvard Theological Review* 83 (1990), p. 449.

Chapter 7

The Basic Structure of Revelation and Its Significance

The structure of a literary work helps determine its meaning. How we say something partly determines what is actually said. Thus, as every writer discovers, usually the two most difficult parts of an essay to compose are the introduction and the conclusion. These are difficult because they are the most important parts of the overall literary structure and so help determine what the essay as a whole means. The reader will expect the introduction to give clues as to what the rest of the work is going to be about and expect the conclusion to repeat the most important points. Consequently, in actual practice, the introduction and conclusion to a surprising degree determine what the work is about and what its major points are. Writers have difficulty composing these passages because the introduction and conclusion shape the whole and so must be fashioned with the rest of the essay in mind lest the reader be misled. In discussing introductions and conclusions, I have merely given an illustration of the larger truth that the way literary material is arranged at least partly determines what its message is. Structure helps determine meaning.

Revelation is tightly structured. An especially striking and pervasive part of that organization is the explicitly numbered sets of sevens that comprise so much of the book. There are seven letters, seven seals, seven trumpets, seven bowls.

Nevertheless, much of Revelation's structure is subtle and complex. Not all the structure is as explicit and straightforward as the great numbered series. We have long passages (e.g., chapters 12-15) that consist of collections of visions in which it is not always obvious even where one vision begins and another ends. In addition, Revelation breaks up ordered sequences. Thus, between the sixth (Rev. 6:12-17) and seventh seal (Rev. 8:1) we have a long interlude. In it 144,000 receive seals on their foreheads (Rev. 7:1-8), and a countless multitude worship God (Rev. 7:9-17). Another complicating feature of Revelation's structure is the parallelism that the book often makes between widely separated blocks of material that occur in very different structural contexts. For example, Revelation makes striking connections between the scene in chapter 5 and the one in chapter 10. Both scenes center around a scroll. Both begin with a "strong angel" (Rev. 5:2, 10:1). Both lead to the unveiling of part of God's plan. Yet these scenes occur in completely opposite structural settings. The first comes immediately *before* the seven seals begin, whereas the second scene takes place *within* the seven trumpets.

Because Revelation's structure is subtle and complex, no outline will ever be definitive, and it may well be that several different ones are necessary to stress different patterns that occur in the book. I offer the following basic outline as a useful structural analysis.

An Outline of Revelation

I. Prologue (1:1-8)
    A. Prophetic preface (1:1-3)
    B. Letter preface (1:4-6)
    C. Sayings (1:7-8)

II. The Seven Letters (1:9-3:22)
    A. Introductory Scene (1:9-20):
        The exalted Christ commands John to write.
    B. The Letters
        1. To Ephesus (2:1-7)
        2. To Smyrna (2:8-11)
        3. To Pergamum (2:12-17)
        4. To Thyatira (2:18-29)
        5. To Sardis (3:1-6)
        6. To Philadelphia (3:7-13)
        7. To Laodicea (3:14-22)

III. The Seven Seals (4:1-8:1)
    A. Introductory Scene (4:1-5:14): God gives the scroll, and the Lamb is able to open it. (For an outline see chapter 10 below.)

B. The Opening of the Seals (6:1-8:1)
    1. The First Seal (6:1-2): The white horse.
    2. The Second Seal (6:3-4): The red horse.
    3. The Third Seal (6:5-6): The black horse.
    4. The Fourth Seal (6:7-8): The green horse.
    5. The Fifth Seal (6:9-11): The martyrs ask, "How long?"
    6. The Sixth Seal (6:12-17): The destruction of this age.
    7. An Interlude that looks forward to chapters 20-21 (7:1-17)
      a. The Sealing of the 144,000 (7:1-8)
      b. The Worship of the Countless Multitude (7:9-17)
    8. The Seventh Seal (8:1): Silence in heaven.

IV. The Seven Trumpets (8:2-11:19)
  A. Introductory Scene (8:2-8:6): The angel and the censer.
  B. The Blowing of the Trumpets (8:7-11:19)
    1. The First Trumpet (8:7): The destruction of a third of the earth.
    2. The Second Trumpet (8:8-9): The destruction of a third of the sea.
    3. The Third Trumpet (8:10-11):
      The destruction of a third of the rivers and springs.
    4. The Fourth Trumpet (8:12):
      The destruction of a third of the sun, moon, and stars.
    5. The Fifth Trumpet [first woe] (8:13-9:12)
      a. Introduction to the Woes (8:13)
      b. The Fifth Trumpet (9:1-12): The monstrous locusts.
    6. The Sixth Trumpet [second woe] (9:13-21)
      a. The hordes from the East kill a third of humankind (9:13-19).
      b. The survivors refuse to repent (9:20-21).
    7. An Interlude that looks forward to chapters 13-15 (10:1-11:13)
      a. John receives and eats the open scroll (10:1-11)
      b. The Two Witnesses (11:1-13)
    8. The Seventh Trumpet [third woe] (11:14-19):
      A heavenly celebration of victory.

V. The First Set of Unnumbered Visions (12:1-14:20)
  A. The Woman and the Dragon (12:1-18)
  B. The Beast from the Sea and the Beast from the Land (13:1-18)
  C. The 144,000 on Mount Zion (14:1-5)
  D. Three Angels Pronounce Judgment (14:6-13)
  E. The Harvesting of the Earth (14:14-20)

VI. The Seven Bowls (15:1-16:21)
 A. Introductory Scene (15:1-16:1):
  The angels prepare to pour out the bowls as the saved praise God.
 B. The Pouring Out of the Bowls (16:2-21)
  1. The First Bowl (16:2): Sores come upon the Beast's followers.
  2. The Second Bowl (16:3): The sea becomes blood.
  3. The Third Bowl (16:4-7): The rivers and springs become blood.
  4. The Fourth Bowl (16:8-9): The sun becomes scorching.
  5. The Fifth Bowl (16:10-11):
   The kingdom of the Beast becomes dark.
  6. The Sixth Bowl (16:12-16):
   The Euphrates is dried up for the kings of the East.
  7. The Seventh Bowl (16:17-21): The destruction of this age.

VII. Babylon (17:1-19:10)
 A. Introduction (17:1-3a): John is led away in the spirit.
 B. The Whore (17:3b-18)
 C. Lamentation over Babylon's Destruction (18:1-24)
 D. Jubilation over Babylon's Destruction (19:1-8)
 E. Conclusion of the Vision:
  John tries to worship the angel who revealed it (19:9-10).

VIII. The Second Set of Unnumbered Visions (19:11-20:15)
 A. The Divine Warrior and His Armies (19:11-16)
 B. The Destruction of the Beast, the False Prophet, and their Followers
  (19:17-21)
 C. The Binding of Satan, the Saints' 1,000-Year Reign, and Satan's Final
  Destruction (20:1-10)
 D. The Judgment of the World (20:11-15)

IX. The New Jerusalem (21:1-22:9)
 A. Introduction: The New Jerusalem descends and John is led away in
  the Spirit (21:1-10).
 B. The City (21:11-22:5)
 C. Conclusion of the Vision:
  John tries to worship the angel who revealed it (22:6-9).

X. Epilogue (22:10-21)
 A. Sayings (22:10-20)
 B. Blessing (22:21)

From this outline, it is clear that the bulk of Revelation is composed of blocks of visions. In addition to the explicitly numbered series of seven letters, seals, trumpets, and bowls, we have two long sets of unnumbered visions.

Within each of these blocks the action moves steadily forward. In the letters we move from one church to the next until we have completed the circuit. In the seals, the trumpets, and the bowls, the destruction increases from one scene to the next until the sinful earth is utterly devastated. In the first set of unnumbered visions the narrative starts with the birth and resurrection of Christ and the expulsion of Satan from heaven (Rev. 12). We go on to the appearance of the two beasts who try to make the whole world worship the first beast (Rev. 13). The 144,000 chosen, however, do not succumb (Rev. 14:1-5). Then three angels announce the fall of Babylon (Rev. 14:6-13). Finally, we have the destruction of this age with the harvesting of the earth (Rev. 14:14-20). So, too, the second set of unnumbered visions proceeds ever forward. We begin with the coming of the divine warrior and his heavenly army (Rev. 19:11-16). They then destroy the beast and his supporters (Rev. 17-21). Satan is bound. The martyrs return to life and reign on earth for a thousand years. Satan is released and rallies his followers for one last assault, but is destroyed (Rev. 20:1-10). The judgment of the world follows.

Structurally, the three cycles of seals, trumpets, and bowls are parallel and stand apart from the rest of the book. Unlike any other section of the Apocalypse, in each of these cycles every vision is numbered separately. Moreover, in the seals and trumpets the seven visions fall naturally into two blocks, namely the first four and the last three. Thus, in the seals the first four visions each concern a colored horse, but the last three do not. In the trumpets the last three visions are separately designated as "three woes" (Rev. 8:13, 9:12, 11:14).

Between the cycles of seals, trumpets, and bowls, there seems to be repetition. Again and again we see essentially the same scene repeated in about the same place. This recapitulation is especially striking between the trumpets and the bowls. Thus, in the second trumpet a third of the sea becomes blood and a third of the creatures in it are destroyed (Rev. 8:8-9). In the second bowl the sea becomes blood and every creature in it is destroyed (Rev. 16:3). In the sixth trumpet (Rev. 9:13-19) we see an army of two hundred million soldiers on monstrous horses at the Euphrates River. These soldiers subsequently kill one-third of humankind. In the sixth bowl (Rev. 16:12-16) an army composed of the kings of the East crosses the dried up Euphrates and gathers at Armageddon for battle. At the seventh trumpet (Rev. 11:15-19) we have a proclamation of final victory, "The kingdom of the world has become the kingdom of our Lord and of his Christ!" (Rev. 11:15). There follows "lightnings and voices and thunders and an earthquake and heavy hail" (Rev. 11:19). At the seventh bowl (Rev. 16:17-21) we also have a proclamation of final victory, "It is done!" (Rev. 16:17). There follows "lightnings and voices and thunders and a great earthquake" (vs. 18) and hail as heavy as a hundred weight (Rev. 16:21). We likewise find parallels between the seals and the other two cycles. The most striking is between the sixth seal and the seventh bowl. In the sixth seal (Rev. 6:12-17) a great earthquake occurs; every island and mountain is removed and people hide in caves to escape the Lamb's wrath. In the seventh bowl (Rev. 16:17-21) a supremely powerful earthquake occurs. The islands and mountains vanish and humankind blasphemes God.

The repetitions between the three numbered series of visions invite the hypothesis that John does not foresee three different sets of events. Instead he foresees only one set but describes it three different times. The technical name for this hypothesis is the "recapitulation theory." The theory appears already in the oldest surviving commentary on Revelation, that of Victorinus of Pettau who was martyred in the year 304, who proposed that the trumpets and the bowls were different presentations of the same prophecy.[1] Since Victorinus' time perhaps the majority of scholars have favored some form of this theory.

In addition to the parallels cited above, a number of considerations lend support to the recapitulation theory. To begin with, the sixth or seventh member of each series is so destructive that we can scarcely imagine how the old age could continue subsequently. For example, when the sixth seal is broken, the sun becomes black, the heavens split open, and the mountains and islands disappear (Rev. 6:12-17). Surely, this must be the end! If such is the case, then the trumpets and bowls cannot be descriptions of cosmic and political disasters that happen *after* the sixth seal. Indeed, some of the things that occur in the trumpets and bowls presuppose that the seals have not taken place. Thus, in the fourth trumpet one-third of the sun becomes dark (Rev. 8:12). Yet in the sixth seal, the entire sun became black (Rev. 6:12)! Another consideration that supports recapitulation is the fact that the last member of each series takes place in heaven and seems to be associated with the final triumph of God.[2] For example, when the seventh trumpet sounds, we have a heavenly proclamation of God's triumph (Rev. 11:15-18), including the words, "The time has come for the dead to be judged." Certainly such a saying must mark the conclusion of this age. The promise of imminent fulfillment in 10:5-7 also demands that the seventh trumpet be the end. The angel's sworn words are solemn and seemingly unambiguous: "There will be no more delay, but in the days of the sound of the seventh angel, who is about to blow the trumpet, the mystery of God will be completed" (Rev. 10:6-7). Without recapitulation the parallels between the seals, trumpets, and bowls become disturbing. For instance, it seems unlikely that John foresaw two demonic invasions across the Euphrates. By contrast, the discrepancies between the three cycles are not necessarily strong evidence against recapitulation. John is a highly poetic and symbolic writer and could have felt free to describe the same event in various ways. A final consideration that strongly supports the idea that the cycles in Revelation represent the same events is that recapitulation is typical of the prophetic and apocalyptic tradition that John and his readers took for granted. In prophetic and apocalyptic works we constantly have very different visions or cycles of visions that forecast the same thing. Amos can see a plumb line (Amos 7:7-9) and later see a basket of summer fruit (Amos 8:1-3). Yet both visions foretell the same coming destruction of Israel. Daniel can first see a leopard with four wings and four heads and another beast with ten horns and iron teeth (Dan. 7:6-7). Subsequently, he can see a he-goat defeat a ram (Dan. 8:1-8). Yet both experiences point to the historical fact that the Greek empire overcame the Persian one.

If there are weighty arguments in favor of recapitulation, there are also weighty arguments against it. The first and most significant is that there is a steady *development* from one cycle to the next. In the fourth seal, a fourth of the earth is destroyed (Rev. 6:8); in the trumpets, a third (Rev. 8:7, 9, etc.); and in the bowls, the whole. Moreover, in 15:1 we are explicitly told that the bowls are "the *last* plagues, because with them the fury of God is ended." The prophetic and apocalyptic traditions commonly use similar images to portray different events. Typology was fundamental to Biblical writing, and depictions of later events are often consciously modeled on earlier ones. John himself clearly bases his presentation of the trumpets and bowls on the ten plagues of Egypt. God of old turned the Nile into blood (Exod. 7:17-21), covered the

Egyptians with boils (Exod. 9:8-10), and sent hail (Exod. 9:18-25), locusts (Exod. 10:4-15), and darkness (Exod. 10:21-23). So, too, in the trumpets and bowls God turns the waters into blood (Rev. 8:8, 16:3-7), covers those who follow the beast with boils (Rev. 16:2), and sends hail (Rev. 8:7, 11:19, 16:21), locusts (Rev. 9:1-11) and darkness (Rev. 8:12, 16:10). Accordingly, merely because John uses similar descriptions need not mean he is describing the same event. Moreover, Revelation provides us with an undeniable illustration of two different events being depicted in the same way. The battle in 20:7-10 *cannot* be the same as the battle in 19:11-21 because the first takes place *after* the thousand-year reign of the saints on earth (Rev. 20:7), whereas the former precedes it. Nevertheless, in both battles we have a final conflict between the forces of this world and those of God, and John employs material taken from Ezekiel 38-39 in both descriptions (Rev. 19:17-18 is based on Ezek. 39:17-20; Rev. 20:8-9 is based on Ezek. 38:2, 22; 39:6)! A final argument against the recapitulation theory is the possibility that the last seal may include the seven trumpets, and the last trumpet may include the seven bowls. This possibility is especially attractive with the seventh seal. When that seal is broken we have half an hour of silence, and then immediately the angels with the seven trumpets appear (Rev. 8:1-2).

The force of the arguments for and against the recapitulation theory suggests that the descriptions in the cycles of seals, trumpets, and bowls are so literary that we should not assume that the individual details are predictive. If we cannot even be certain whether the three cycles portray one series of future events or three, we can scarcely be certain of anything. Accordingly, the details of the seals, trumpets, and bowls should not be pressed to yield specific forecasts. The details come from John's need to make dramatic scenes and use preexistent material. Thus, it is primarily in order to create an increasing sense of drama that John makes the destruction in the seals be one fourth of the earth, that in the trumpets, one third, and that in the bowls, the whole. Similarly, it is in order to honor his biblical heritage and remain part of it, that John uses the plagues of Egypt as the model for the trumpets and bowls. The details in the cycles arise out of literary and devotional needs and should not be tortured into providing some coherent and complex scheme of events for the end time.

Instead, we should consider the hypothesis that the seals and trumpets and bowls are only making a single basic prediction. Under the profusion of images and scenes there is only one simple forecast whose details are either unknown or unimportant. That simple forecast was so wonderful and crucial that John felt no one set of images could do it justice, and, therefore, he resorted to the great cycles that appear in his book. If this hypothesis is correct, the angel's solemn promise that there would be no more delay becomes comprehensible (Rev. 10:6).

If we now turn to the unnumbered visions, we see at once that the two sets seem linear rather than repetitive. Whereas in the seals, trumpets, and bowls the same material often appears in about the same place in each cycle, the second set of unnumbered visions seems to commence where the first set leaves off. Thus, at the end of the first set we have a cataclysmic scene (Rev. 14:14-20). "One like a son of humanity" (Rev. 14:14) followed by an angel harvests the earth, and, as a result, blood flows for 1600 stadia (300 kilometers). At the beginning of the second set of visions we have a cataclysmic scene (Rev. 19:11-21) in which the "Word of God" (vs. 13) followed by his troops destroys the kings of the earth with their armies, and the birds become gorged with flesh. It is noteworthy that both scenes talk about the wine press of God's fury (Rev. 14:19, 19:15). The parallelism between the scenes becomes even greater when we remember that, for John and his intended readers, the "one like a son of humanity" and the "Word of God" were both titles referring to Jesus.

If we combine the two sets of unnumbered visions, we have a continuous narrative of events from the birth of Jesus until the final consummation. In the first set of visions we begin with the birth of the messiah and his entrance into heaven. As a result, Satan is cast out. The devil comes down to earth and rouses up a beast from the sea and one from the land. These force everyone except the elect to worship the image of the first beast. However, we get a glimpse of 144,000 faithful. Three angels announce the doom of those who worship the beast. There is a gruesome harvest of the earth. In the second set of visions we start with the destruction of the beast and his supporters. The martyrs return to life and reign for a millennium. Satan organizes one last assault, but he and his supporters are destroyed. Subsequently, there is a general resurrection and judgment.

Despite the fact that the two sets of unnumbered visions taken together form a continuous linear narrative, these visions also have structural anomalies. For example, the opening of the first set is full of problems. In 12:1-6 Satan pursues a woman who gives birth to the Messiah and who then flees into the wilderness. Yet in verses 7-8 Satan is back in heaven and must be cast down to earth. Once there he again pursues the woman who again flees into the wilderness (Rev. 12:13-14). A striking literary anomaly in the second set of visions is the enormous disparity in the amount of space John devotes to the otherwise similar battles in chapters 19 and 20. As noted above, in content the battles are basically the same. Yet John spends eleven verses describing the first engagement (Rev. 19:11-21) and only four (Rev. 20:7-10) on the second.

As in the case of the three sets of numbered visions, literary rather than theological needs seem to have dictated many of the specific details in the unnumbered sequences. Once again, John labors to incorporate traditional images and scenes and struggles to make his narrative dramatic. Thus, much of the material in chapter 12 is derived from pagan mythology, and perhaps John drew on this anti-Christian material for artistic effect. The story of a dragon pursuing a woman who flees into the wilderness and gives birth to a male child that slays the monster goes all the way back to Near Eastern creation myths. The form of the tale John and his readers knew concerned the birth of the God Apollo. Since Apollo was a divine patron of the emperor, perhaps John revised the material in order to drive home to his readers that Christ — not Apollo and the emperors — is the one who really slays the monster of evil. Similarly, one reason that the battle scene in Rev. 20:7-10 is so short is that John probably had a literary need to press on to the climax of the book, which is the description of the New Jerusalem. Once the beast is destroyed in chapter 19, John had to conclude rapidly or else the reader would begin to lose interest. As a result, John hastened to begin his description of the final consummation and quickly passed over all preliminaries.

Because of John's literary concerns one cannot be sure that the details in the unnumbered visions should be seen as predictions of the future. Thus, it is possible — but by no means certain — that John believed that the resurrected martyrs would literally reign on earth prior to the general resurrection. Perhaps, like the author of II Esdras, John believed that there would be a fulfillment of both the Old Testament promises of an earthly messianic reign and the promises of a new heaven and earth (II Esdras 7:26-44). Perhaps, however, John merely wanted to honor traditional material, and the thousand-year reign of the saints on earth is no more to be taken literally than the demonic locusts that materialize from the shaft of the abyss in the fifth trumpet.

Accordingly, as with the numbered cycles, we may suspect that the unnumbered visions predict a relatively simple set of chronological events. Under the wealth of images and traditional material and stunning literary effects there is only a basic forecast.

Revelation has long sections on Babylon and Jerusalem (Rev. 17:1-19:10; 21:1-22:9). Each of these two sections has a special introduction that tells how John entered into the spirit and where the vision took place (Rev. 17:1-3, 21:1-10). These introductions separate the visions from the previous material and so make them independent units.

The sections on Babylon and Jerusalem have striking parallels. Later we will review these parallels in detail (see chapter 11 below). Here we will only note that some of the opening words of each section are identical: "One of the seven angels who had the seven bowls came and spoke with me saying, 'Come, I will show you,'" but after these opening words we have the starkest contrast imaginable. In the one case the angel announces he will show the "judgment of the great whore" (Rev. 17:1), whereas in the other case the angel promises to show "the bride, the wife of the Lamb" (Rev. 21:9).

The structural parallelism between Babylon and the New Jerusalem indicates that part of Revelation's basic message is the contrast between the two cities. By isolating the units about the two cities from the surrounding cycles of visions, the structure invites us to consider the two cities together. By giving verbally similar introductions that lead to very different descriptions, the structure invites us to contrast Babylon and the New Jerusalem.

The repeated previews of the New Jerusalem and the placement of the section itself strongly suggest that this unit is the climax of the book. Throughout Revelation we have foretastes of this section. For example, in the letter to Ephesus we have a reference to the tree of life (Rev. 2:7), which we later discover is in the New Jerusalem (Rev. 22:2), and in the letter to Philadelphia we hear about "the city of my God, the new Jerusalem" (Rev. 3:12). These foretastes whet our appetites and so make the final description of Jerusalem all the more powerful. The placement of the section as the last major unit also makes it a high point. After the description of Jerusalem we have only a few concluding remarks. Of course, the reader naturally expects the last sustained passage to be especially important.

Let us now summarize the basic conclusions we have reached about Revelation's structure and its significance. In addition to the preface and epilogue, Revelation consists of four blocks of material: 1) the letters to the seven churches, 2) three sets of numbered visions that repeat the same basic material, 3) two sets of unnumbered visions which present a continuous narrative, and 4) two independent but parallel sections about Babylon and the New Jerusalem. Because the three cycles of numbered visions repeat much of the same material, they probably present a single message under a variety of images. Because the two sets of unnumbered visions taken together form a continuous narrative, but the narrative has anomalies, the unnumbered visions may predict a simple series of chronological events. The fact that the section describing the New Jerusalem occurs near the end of the book and contrasts with the section on Babylon suggests that John wanted his readers to focus on the New Jerusalem and see its superiority to "Babylon."

Appendix: The Numerology of Revelation

Revelation has a few passages in which numbers do not seem to have any numerological significance. In these occasional passages the numbers are due to other factors such as John's use of sources. Thus, the fact that there are *four* living creatures (Rev. 4:6) around the throne and each has *six* wings (4:8) seems to be due to the influence of Isaiah and Ezekiel. John produced the creatures by combining the six-winged seraphim that accompany God in Isaiah's inaugural vision (Isa. 6:2) and the four four-faced creatures that accompany God in Ezekiel's (Ez. 1:5-11). The result was *four* creatures that have *six* wings each.

For the most part, however, the numbers in Revelation seem to be due to numerology. John attributed different symbolic significance to different numbers. Hence, he used particular numbers in particular contexts.

Basically, we must deduce this numerology from Revelation itself. Perhaps John borrowed his whole numerological system. However, if he did, we do not have the source. The only source we *know* that John used heavily is the Old Testament. Hence, all we can do is see how he used numbers and note when he seems to have taken a particular usage from the scriptures.

Clearly, for John the most important number is seven, and it signifies completion. Normally, "seven" of something is all of them. The seventh seal, trumpet, or bowl completes the series. Interestingly enough, John can use seven both in descriptions of good and evil. Thus, the Lamb has seven horns (Rev. 5:6) and the Beast seven heads (Rev. 13:1). John got the idea that seven signifies completion from the Old Testament, especially the seven days of creation in Genesis 1.

By contrast, six and three and one-half signify incompleteness and, therefore, evil. Six falls one short of the perfect number and is associated with rebellion against God. The number of the Beast is 666 (Rev. 13:18), and John is living during the reign of the sixth (Rev. 17:10) emperor. Three and one-half is half of seven and is associated with tribulation. The corpses of the faithful witnesses lie unburied for three and one-half days (Rev. 11:11), and the Beast will wield authority for forty-two months or three and one-half years (Rev. 13:5). Presumably John derived the idea that three and one-half is the appropriate number for a period of tribulation from Daniel (Dan. 7:25, 12:7).

John also has a series of numbers that seem to refer to various types of fullness. Four appears to represent the fullness of the earth. Thus, at one point John mentions *four* winds (Rev. 7:1). Apparently, John derived this numerological convention from the four directions of the compass (cf. Rev. 21:13). Ten represents the fullness of evil or tribulation. Thus, the Beast has ten horns (Rev. 13:1), and the church at Smyrna will suffer for ten days (Rev. 2:10). Twelve represents the number of fullness of good. Hence, the number of those sealed from each tribe of Israel is twelve thousand (Rev. 7:4-8). This numerological convention goes back to the twelve tribes of Israel and the twelve apostles (see Rev. 21:12-14). Finally, one thousand represents the fullness of large numbers.

An interesting feature of Revelation is that multiples and especially the square of a number have the same basic properties as the number itself. Hence, John tells us the wall of the new Jerusalem is 144 (i.e., 12 x 12) cubits high (Rev. 21:17).

If we remember that for John numbers are largely symbolic and, therefore, need not be taken literally, certain potential theological and exegetical problems disappear. "144,000," which is the number of the sealed from the tribes of Israel (Rev. 7:4-8) and the number of those who stood with the Lamb on Zion (Rev. 14:1), does not limit the elect. On the contrary, since twelve and one thousand are both numbers indicating fullness, 144,000 indicates that all Israel will be saved. "The seven spirits" of God (e.g., Rev. 4:5) need not refer to seven angelic beings but to the completeness of the Holy Spirit.[3] The "1260 days" of tribulation (e.g., Rev. 12:6) or the "1,000 years" of the saints reigning on earth (Rev. 20:4-7) probably are not to be taken literally but merely indicate that the tribulation will be brief and the reign long.

Notes

[1]Victorinus makes this observation in the section of his commentary that deals with Revelation 7. For the text, see Alexander Roberts and James Donaldson, eds., *The Ante-Nicene Fathers*, vol. vii (Grand Rapids: Eerdmans, 1867), p. 352.

[2]There can be no doubt that the seventh trumpet and bowl proclaim the triumph of God (Rev. 11:15-18; 16:17). The significance of the half an hour of silence that occurs at the seventh seal is less clear (Rev. 8:1).

[3]In my opinion, two things preclude the possibility that these seven spirits can be anything other than the fullness of the Holy Spirit. First, in 1:4-5, John places the seven spirits between the Father and the Son and so indicates that these "spirits" are on the same level as God and Jesus. Second, the seven eyes of the Lamb are said to be the seven spirits (Rev. 5:6). It is much easier to think of Jesus being filled with the Holy Spirit than with seven heavenly beings!

Chapter 8

The Basic Message of Revelation

In this chapter we will test an hypothesis concerning the basic message of Revelation, which is based on the structural analysis of the previous chapter. We will then test the hypothesis by seeing if it can clarify the passage concerning the two witnesses (Rev. 11:1-13). This passage is a good test case because it has been a continuing puzzle even to specialists on the Apocalypse. Indeed, as one scholar noted, "The views about the function and structure of this passage are as numerous as the commentaries."[1]

In the last chapter we saw that the body of Revelation consists of four basic complexes. If we set aside the preface and the epilogue, we have the letters to the churches (Rev. 1:9-3:22), the three numbered cycles of visions (namely, the seals, trumpets, and bowls of Rev. 4:1-11:19 and 15:1-16:21), the two unnumbered cycles of visions (Rev. 12:1-14:20 and 19:11-20:15) and the parallel sections on Babylon (Rev. 17:1-19:10) and the New Jerusalem (Rev. 21:1-22:9).

We also saw that the basic messages of these sections are probably simple. The kaleidoscopic details of the book are due at least in part to John's need to honor his tradition and produce dramatic scenes. Hence, we should not assume that John is making a complex set of predictions or admonitions. Instead it is likely that his forecasts and exhortations are basically simple.

The fundamental message of the seven letters is clear: The churches should repent of their sins and stand firm in their virtues because a decisive time is coming. Each of the letters contains admonitions. The basis of the admonitions is the claim that those who heed John's warnings will be protected and come to eternal blessings, whereas those who do not will be destroyed. For example, in the letter to the Philadelphians Christ commends the congregation for keeping his word (Rev. 3:8) and exhorts them to hold on to what they have (Rev.

3:11). Jesus promises to keep them from the "hour of testing which is about to come on the whole world" (Rev. 3:10). He also declares that he will come soon (vs. 11), and those who remain faithful will inherit the New Jerusalem (Rev. 3:12).

The basic message of the seals, trumpets, and bowls is that there will be an escalating set of cosmic and political woes that will culminate in catastrophe. These woes are to punish the godless and warn them to repent. Thus, in each of the cycles we have a series of social and natural calamities such as war (Rev. 6:3-4) or one-third of the sea turning to blood (Rev. 8:8). Finally, we have a nightmarish invasion from the East (Rev. 9:13-19, 16:12-16) followed by cosmic collapse (Rev. 6:12-17, 16:17-21). In recounting them, Revelation makes it clear that these horrors will come upon the godless to chastise them. In the fifth seal (Rev. 6:9-11) the martyred saints cry for vengeance, and the catastrophic sixth seal seems to be God's response. Similarly, the demonic locusts of the fifth trumpet (Rev. 9:1-11) are ordered not to attack "the grass of the earth, nor any green thing, nor any tree, only people who do not have the seal of God upon their foreheads" (Rev. 9:4). Accordingly, the locusts torment the godless for five months (Rev. 9:5). An additional purpose for these scourges is to summon human beings to repentance. On the whole, people do not repent, but it is noteworthy that John repeatedly stresses this failing and so calls attention to God's summons. Indeed, the words "they blasphemed God" and "did not repent" are almost a refrain in the cycle of bowls (Rev. 16:9, 16:11, 16:21).

In order to discover the fundamental message of the two sets of unnumbered visions, we must review the basic narrative. A celestial woman gives birth to a child who is caught up into heaven. Satan is cast out of heaven and pursues the woman, but she manages to flee and so is saved. Satan then goes off to fight against the woman's other children. He rouses up two beasts, one from the sea and one from the land. The second forces the whole world to worship the first, and anyone who refuses is put to death. Consequently, many who are faithful to the Lamb die. Then there is a fearful judgment. In the first set of unnumbered visions the judgment occurs when "one like a son of humanity" (Rev. 14:14) and an angel harvest the earth. In the second set the judgment occurs when the "Word of God" (Rev. 19:13) slays the armies of the world. The Beast and False Prophet (i.e., the beast from the land) are slain, Satan is bound, and the martyrs rise from the dead and reign for a thousand years. Satan organizes a final assault and is destroyed. All the dead are raised and judged, and the wicked are cast into the lake of fire.

Happily, the meaning of the major symbols in the narrative is readily apparent. The woman is the continuing people of God, and thus stands for both the old and new Israel (i.e., the Christian church). The Beast from the Sea is the Roman Emperors, and in chapter 17 we are explicitly told that its seven heads represent the individual rulers (Rev. 17:9). The head that had a deadly wound is Nero, who had been assassinated and subsequently was rumored to be alive. The Beast from the Land represents the local authorities who enforce worshipping the emperor. The one "like a son of humanity" and the "Word of God" are Jesus.

Consequently, the basic message of the unnumbered visions is that there will soon be a final catastrophic imperial persecution, and then God will judge the world. For some time after Christ's resurrection there had been persecution, but the church survived. To use the imagery of Revelation, Satan pursued the woman and tried to destroy her, but she escaped. Soon, however, there will be a devastating imperial persecution. The emperor assisted by local authorities will compel everyone to worship the imperial image, and anyone who refuses will be put to death. As a result, many Christians will perish. Shortly thereafter God will destroy the world, judge the dead, and reward everyone in accordance with their works. As we noted in the last chapter, it is hard to know whether some of the individual episodes (e.g., the millennium) in the unnumbered visions should be pressed to yield a detailed forecast.

The thrust of the parallel visions concerning "Babylon" and the New Jerusalem is that Rome is evil and will soon be destroyed, whereas the coming kingdom of God is unimaginably glorious and will last forever. In his depiction of the first city, John stresses its sleaze and transitoriness. Babylon is a whore and is drunk with the blood of the saints (Rev. 17:4-6). In one hour she will be utterly laid waste (e.g., Rev. 18:17, 19). By contrast, the New Jerusalem is a pure bride of unspeakable magnificence, and in her God's saints will reign forever and ever (Rev. 22:5).

Earlier we noted that normally the introduction and conclusion of a book encapsulate the central message. The introduction shapes how the reader approaches the rest of the material. Consequently, the introduction should provide the author's basic framework in which the details can be properly placed. The conclusion as the closing unit shapes how the reader remembers the rest of the material and so should reaffirm the basic point to which the details contribute.

The introduction and conclusion of Revelation stress that the reader must remain faithful because soon God will definitely judge the world and reward the righteous and destroy the wicked. Thus, the introduction insists, "Blessed is the one who reads aloud and those who hear the words of the prophecy and keep what is written in it because the time is near" (Rev. 1:3) and "Look, he is coming with the clouds" (Rev. 1:7). The conclusion stresses the same theme and even uses much of the same language. "Look, I am coming quickly. Blessed is the one who keeps the words of the prophecy of this book" (Rev. 22:7). "My reward is with me to recompense to each in accordance with their work" (Rev. 22:12).

On the basis of what we have seen we can set out the message of Revelation. Christians must at present more than ever before remain faithful. Up to this time God's judgments and the church's tribulations have been only mild, and so the church has endured and even prospered. However, God will soon send an ever more dire series of cosmic catastrophes that will punish the wicked and challenge them to repent. At the same time there will be an imperial persecution of unprecedented proportions that will decimate the church. Then the end of this age will come. Rome will be destroyed; the cosmos will collapse. Christ will raise the martyrs to eternal glory and then judge the world.

We can be confident that this reconstruction of Revelation's message is correct because on the basis of it we can convincingly unlock the meaning of the problematic scene concerning the two witnesses in Rev. 11:1-13. In the opening verses John tells us that he measured the sanctuary and the altar but not the outer court because it would be trampled by the Gentiles. For John the temple symbolized the church, and the Gentiles, the church's persecutors. The message is that in the first period of church history there will be persecutions, but the church as a whole will endure. Then in verses 3-13 John tells us about the two witnesses whom John compares to two olive trees and two lampstands. There is here a clear allusion to Zechariah 4 where the high priest Joshua (Zech. 3:1ff.) and the royal Zerubbabel (Zech. 4:6ff.) are called two olive trees (Zech. 4:11) standing beside a lampstand (Zech. 4:3, 4:11). Hence, it seems likely that for John the two figures represent royal and priestly testimony to Jesus and that therefore the figures symbolize the church, which elsewhere John calls a kingdom of priests (Rev. 1:6, 5:10, 20:6). If we follow what happens to the two witnesses in

Revelation 11, we see it corresponds exactly with John's vision of what has happened and will happen to the church. Thus, the two witnesses prophesy with impunity for 1260 days (Rev. 11:3), and during that period they call down plagues on the earth (Rev. 11:5-6). So, too, during the first period of church history the Christian community has God's protection and testifies against the world. In its testimony the church interprets the cosmic disasters that God is bringing on the world. At the end of their testimony the Beast ascends from the abyss and kills the witnesses (Rev. 11:7), but three and a half days later they come to life and ascend into heaven (Rev. 11:11-12). So, too, John anticipates a terrible time of tribulation when the church will be decimated. However, that period will be brief. God will quickly intervene and raise the martyrs to glory. Finally, as the witnesses ascend into heaven, there is a great earthquake and their persecutors become terrified (Rev. 11:13). So, too, part of John's basic message is that God will destroy this present age and those who did evil will suffer His wrath.

The structure of Revelation gives further evidence that our reconstruction of the meaning of the two witnesses section is accurate. Structurally, the two witnesses section is part of a long interlude (Rev. 10:1-11:13) that occurs within the seven trumpets and looks forward to the first set of unnumbered visions. In the interlude an angel gives John a book and tells him he must "prophecy again" (Rev. 10:11). As we saw earlier, the basic message of the trumpets is that God is sending a set of increasing natural and social disasters that will decimate the wicked and culminate in cosmic catastrophe. The basic message of the first set of unnumbered visions is that the church is experiencing increasing persecution that shortly will be devastating. Resurrection and judgment will follow. Literarily, a forward looking interlude serves as a bridge passage and so ideally should summarize previous material and preview what is to come. Significantly, as our interpretation makes clear, the two witnesses section does indeed do both.

From our reconstruction of Revelation's message we can see that basically John has merely updated older Christian teaching. When John was writing around the end of Domitian's reign, the idea that there would be increasing cosmic disaster and governmental persecution shortly before the end of this present world had long been commonplace in church teaching. For example, the Gospel of Mark, which was written around the year 70, presents the same schema. In chapter 13 we read that first there will be wars and earthquakes and famines (Mark 13:7-8), and Christians will suffer various persecutions on account of the gospel (Mark 13:9-13). But the end is not yet. Then, however, there will be a "devastating sacrilege" (Mark 13:14) including unparalleled suffering (Mark 13:17-20) and the appearance of false prophets (Mark 13:21-22). Shortly thereafter, "the powers of heaven will be shaken" (Mark 13:24-25), and Christ will return in glory and raise his elect (Mark 13:26-27). Basically, all John has done in Revelation is take this traditional timetable concerning the end and update it by incorporating the events and expectations of his own day. For Mark the final catastrophe preceding the end was the destruction of Jerusalem; for John the final catastrophe was the expected imperial persecution under Domitian and Nero's expected invasion from the East.

Accordingly, we cannot dismiss Revelation's theology as an aberration. Superficially Revelation seems to be very different from the other books of the New Testament, because Revelation clothes its message in fantastic imagery. Basically, however, Revelation's predictions are the same as those of the first three gospels. Even John's updating of earlier apocalyptic forecasts has close parallels in other New Testament books. For example, Luke, who also wrote some years later than Mark, updates Mark's forecasts. Luke used Mark as one of his sources, and Luke 21 takes over much of Mark 13. Yet Luke dates the second coming long after the destruction of Jerusalem. First the times of the Gentiles must be fulfilled (Luke 21:24).

If the basic message of Revelation is the same as that of other New Testament writings, the question of whether that message is true becomes crucial. Since Revelation's theology resembles that found in such books as Mark and Luke, we cannot dismiss Revelation and cling to the gospels. If Revelation is false, then so are Mark and Luke. Accordingly, it is essential for us to discover what Revelation's message rests on and whether that message is in fact true. To the first of these problems we now turn.

Notes

[1]Allan McNicol, "Revelation 11:1-14 and the Structure of the Apocalypse," *Restoration Quarterly* 22 (1979), p. 194.

PART III

The Spiritual Basis of Revelation's Message

Chapter 9

John's Invitation
to Judge His Visions From the Inside

Even in comparison with relatively similar works like Daniel and I Enoch, Revelation's style is highly distinctive. Despite the fact that John employs many of the same literary devices, he departs from his tradition in significant ways. To begin with, John makes his allegories less transparent. A number of other "apocalyptic" works — including Daniel and I Enoch — contain allegories. The supposed authors of these writings have visions that present history by means of a code language. Sometimes animals stand for nations and horns for individual rulers. Thus, at one point "Daniel" has a vision in which a he-goat with one great horn tramples a ram; then the great horn is shattered and four horns replace it (Dan. 8:5-8). This vision foretells that the Greeks under Alexander the Great will destroy the Persian empire and that subsequently Alexander will die and four successors will divide up his territory. As this illustration suggests, in works like Daniel and I Enoch, the meaning of the allegories is absolutely clear. Not only do the allegories retell events that were familiar to the original readers, in addition, after the allegories are over, the books sometimes provide interpretations that systematically decode the symbols. Thus, after the allegory of the ram and the he-goat in Daniel, we are explicitly told that the ram is the "kings of Media and Persia" (Dan. 8:20), the he-goat "the king of Greece" (Dan. 8:21) and so forth.[1] By contrast, the allegories of John's apocalypse are more mysterious. In part this greater sense of mystery comes from the fact that Revelation does not retell past events. Since Revelation is not pseudonymous, there is no need for retrospective "prophecy." In part, however, this greater sense of mystery seems deliberate. Revelation makes the reader do more work. Instead of elaborate interpretations of the allegories, we get only snippets (the longest is Rev. 17:7-18). We are told that the number of the Beast is the number of a human being and is 666 (Rev. 13:18), that "the seven heads are seven mountains where the woman is seated and seven kings" (Rev. 17:9), and the woman is the "great city" (Rev. 17:18). But that is about all. Moreover, Revelation insists that we must think for ourselves. Before telling us the number of the Beast, Revelation announces, "This calls for wisdom" (Rev. 13:18). Before telling us about the seven heads, Revelation announces, "This calls for a mind which has understanding" (Rev. 17:9). Whereas Daniel simply informs us the he-goat is Greece, Revelation makes us conclude for ourselves that the Beast is the emperors and the city is Rome. In addition to providing less explicit interpretative material, Revelation sometimes makes symbols more mysterious by generalizing. Occasionally the same symbol refers to more than one thing. The seven heads of the Beast in chapter 17 represent both seven hills and seven kings (Rev. 17:9). The Beast itself represents both the entire line of emperors and the individual ruler Nero (e.g., Rev. 17:8-13). At times symbols represent not only specific things but larger spiritual categories. The Beast in chapter 13 includes features of each of the four beasts in Daniel 7 and so seems to represent not only the Roman empire but every evil empire. The "Great City" that can be called "Sodom and Egypt" is also the place where Jesus was crucified (Rev. 11:8) and so stands not just for Rome but for every oppressive city.[2] Because Revelation gives us less to go on and often generalizes, some of the visions such as the one in Rev. 11:1-13, were probably challenging to the first readers and certainly remain challenging today.

Another striking difference between Revelation and books like Daniel and I Enoch is that Revelation is tightly organized. These other works are very loosely structured. Thus, Daniel is very diverse. Part of the book is in Aramaic (Dan. 2:4-7:28) and the rest in Hebrew. The book's first half consists of a series of traditional stories about Daniel and his friends surviving ordeals in ancient Babylon, whereas the last half consists of visions in which Daniel foresees subsequent history. Because books like Daniel have such a loose structure, it would be possible to add or remove individual sections without disrupting the composition as a whole. Perhaps as a result, a number of "apocalypses" (e.g., I Enoch) have been heavily edited over the centuries. By contrast, as we saw above in chapter 7, Revelation is very carefully structured. Much of the book consists of series of sevens—seven letters to churches, seven seals, seven trumpets, seven bowls; and, for the most part, these series repeat the same basic themes. However, from one series to the next there is intensification. Thus, in one of the seals we read that one-fourth of the earth was destroyed (Rev. 6:8), whereas in the trumpets one-third of each category is destroyed, and in the bowls everything is obliterated. There is also intensification within the series. Each of the scenes is more dramatic than the last. We may use the seven seals to illustrate. The seals begin with the famous four horses (Rev. 6:1-8). Each horse is a more ominous color white, red, black, and green[3] and brings a greater degree of destruction. In the fifth seal we hear the souls of the martyrs praying for God to take final vengeance on "those who dwell on the earth" (Rev. 6:10). In the sixth seal the world lurches toward collapse. Among other disasters the sun becomes black, every mountain and island is removed, and people hide among the rocks (Rev. 6:12-17). Then, in order to increase the suspense even more, John inserts an interlude in which the saints are sealed. Only after we have waited breathlessly during a whole chapter for the seventh seal does it finally get broken (Rev. 8:1), and then all that happens is half an hour of silence, and we are immediately plunged into the seven trumpets.

So tight is the organization of Revelation and so important is it to John that he takes a special step to prevent someone from adding or deleting anything. At the end of his book he pronounces a solemn warning to all who would alter the text. Those who insert anything will inherit the plagues Revelation so powerfully describes, and those who remove anything will lose their share in the tree of life and the holy city (Rev. 22:18-19).

Despite the unparalleled tightness of Revelation's structure, the book manages to produce sustained waves of images that are more gripping than in any other apocalypse. To study how John builds up a scene we may use as an example the devastating description of the fiery locusts in the fifth trumpet. Whereas the other "apocalypses" tend to place only a few images (often stereotypical ones at that) side by side, Revelation piles powerful images together to produce stunning effects. As Revelation tells us that the locusts have golden crowns, human faces, women's hair, lion's teeth, iron breastplates, and tails of scorpions (Rev. 9:7-10), we conjure up an image of a monster that is awesome in its fearfulness and yet, strange to say, somehow credible.

Despite the unparalleled tightness of Revelation's structure, Revelation also has almost kaleidoscopic changes of location and speaker. Sometimes even within the same short literary unit the text jumps without warning from one place to another, from one time to another, from one speaker to another. Indeed, in the literarily important concluding verses (Rev. 22:6-21) the speaker changes so often that we are not always certain who the speaker is. As an example of sudden changes in location and speaker we may glance at the section concerning the third bowl.

> And the third angel poured out his bowl into the rivers and the fountains of waters, and they became blood, and I heard the angel of the waters saying, "Righteous are you, who is and who was, the holy one, because you have made these judgments. Because they poured out the blood of saints and prophets, and you have given to them blood to drink. They are deserving!" And I heard the altar saying, "Yes, Lord God, the almighty; true and righteous are your judgments!" (Rev. 16:4-7)

Here in one very brief, coherent literary unit we move from heaven to earth and back to heaven, and we have sudden comments from the previously unmentioned "angel of the waters" and the previously silent altar!

Like his kaleidoscopic changes of location and speaker, John's innovative use of scripture produces additional excitement.   John constantly adapts the Old Testament. Again and again he reminds us of a sacred text and yet, at the same time, surprises us by doing something new with it. The reminiscences give Revelation a pervasive sense of holiness and solemnity while John's changes supply a special dramatic edge. As an illustration of John's technique, we may look at how he adapts Daniel 12:4. In Daniel 12:4 an angel commands Daniel to seal up the prophetic words until the distant endtime. By contrast, in Revelation an angel commands John, "Do *not* seal up the words of the prophecy . . . for the time is near" (Rev. 22:10). Here John makes us think back on Daniel 12:4 even as he reverses it.   Consequently, the saying in Revelation has both a solemnity and freshness that are breathtaking.

Still another stylistic difference between Revelation and the historical apocalypses is that Revelation admonishes the reader directly. In part this difference is due to the dropping of pseudonymity. In the other apocalypses pseudonymity made direct address difficult. As a result, even though at least many of these books (e.g., Daniel) were intended to be admonitions, they generally do not in fact contain explicit ones. By dropping pseudonymity John was able to address the reader directly.   John's admonitions are systematically incorporated into the text. Thus, the seven letters present specific warnings or commendations to each congregation by name, along with the general refrain, "Let those who have ears hear what the spirit is saying to the churches." In later sections of the Apocalypse John suddenly breaks into direct admonitions at key points. For example, in the middle of the description of the great persecution in chapter 13 John abruptly adds, "If anyone has an ear, let them hear" (Rev. 13:9). A long admonition follows (vs. 10).

Because of all the stylistic differences between Revelation and the other apocalypses, the overall effect of Revelation is fundamentally different. In the other apocalypses the visions remain someone else's, whereas in Revelation they become our own. When one reads, say, Daniel or I Enoch, one remains basically uninvolved in the scenes. There is a distance between the reader and the material. The reader sits back and considers someone else's visions. For example, if the vision contains an allegory, the reader sits back and systematically decodes it. By contrast, Revelation draws the reader into the scenes. The tight organization and careful progression create excitement and expectation. The powerful waves of imagery inspire wonder and terror. John's innovative use of familiar scriptural texts and his sudden changes in speaker, time, and location keep us alert. The sense of mystery that pervades the allegories and often appears elsewhere prevents us from becoming too comfortable. The admonitions address us directly and call forth hope, repentance, and commitment. As a result, the reader becomes involved.

We now can see at least one way that Revelation tries to make its message credible: Revelation invites readers to experience the visions, and the visions are self-authenticating. Revelation invites us to make its visions our own. We are summoned to see and hear what John saw and heard. John's hope is that, like him, we will be so overwhelmed by the power of the experience that we will not doubt that the visions come from God and reveal the truth.

Notes

[1]Another readily available illustration of an elaborate animal allegory followed by an interpretation occurs in II Esdras 11:1-12:35, which is in the Apocrypha.

[2]C. B. Caird, *A Commentary on the Revelation of St. John the Divine* (London: Adam & Charles Black, 1966), pp. 137-138.

[3]I prefer the translation "green" to "pale." The Greek word can mean either, but "green" is the more common meaning and is the meaning elsewhere in Revelation (Rev. 8:7, 9:4). In this passage "green" suggests gangrene.

Chapter 10

The Nature of God and the Deeds of the Lamb

Like other apocalypses Revelation is composed mostly of visions, and, indeed, the bulk of the book consists of four great visionary cycles. In Revelation we have four special introductions that tell us that John entered into the spirit and which even give the location in which the vision occurred. Each of the introductions then leads directly into a large block of visionary material. Specifically, in the first visionary introduction John tells us how he "entered into the spirit" while he was on Patmos (Rev. 1:9-10). Subsequently, we have the great vision of Christ walking among the lampstands and dictating the seven letters to the churches (Rev. 1:10-3:22). In the second introduction John tells us how he "entered into the spirit" and ascended through an open door into heaven (Rev. 4:1-2). We then get the vision of the worship of God and the Lamb that in turn leads directly into the seven seals. In the third introduction John in the spirit is carried away into the wilderness (Rev. 17:3) and subsequently we have the great vision of Babylon and its fall (Rev. 17:3-18:24). Finally, in the fourth preface John in the spirit alights on a great high mountain (Rev. 21:10) from where he sees the New Jerusalem which he then describes so movingly (Rev. 21:11-22:5).

In recounting his visions John makes the claim that he has had privileged access to heavenly mysteries and, therefore, can reveal them. Thanks to God's special dispensation John has been able to behold things that are hidden from other human beings. Hence, he has the right and obligation to make known God's will to the church. Already in the opening sentence John insists that God has shown him things which he passes on to us, "The revelation of Jesus Christ which God gave to him to show to his servants what must take place quickly, and he made it known by sending it through his angel to his servant John" (1:1).

Of course, other biblical visionaries had made similar claims. The Old Testament prophets, for example, saw visions and claimed that consequently they had received special insight into the judgments of

God. It was, therefore, both the prophet's right and duty to make this privileged knowledge available to others.

There are at least two possible ways to back up the claim that through a vision one has received special insight into God's will; John chose the second. On the one hand, one can appeal to the credentials of the visionary. In general the apocalypses did this. The vision had to be trustworthy because the figure who had it was authoritative. Since Enoch or Daniel or Ezra were exemplary saints of old who enjoyed a special relationship with God, and since their word was fulfilled in the past, any visions that they had about our future must be reliable. On the other hand, one can appeal to the persuasiveness of the vision itself. The vision is so enlightening, so moving, so inspiring that when it is recounted, those who hear cannot doubt that it is true. As we have seen, Revelation appeals to the persuasiveness of the vision rather than the credentials of the visionary. John wrote under his own name and made no claims about himself. Instead, he presents the visions so powerfully that we are drawn into them, they become our visions, and we recognize their truth.

Interestingly, one particular vision — that in chapters 4-5 — seems to deal almost explicitly with the crucial question of how John could know the future. These chapters concern the problem of opening the scroll that contains a record of coming events. John beholds the scroll, but it cannot be read. The writing is on the inside and the back, and the document is sealed. He is then challenged with the vital question of who can open the book. Significantly, the scene occurs immediately before the first major predictive visions and prepares for them. As noted above, chapters 4-5 are the introduction for at least the seven seals and perhaps for the following visions as well. The seals and the subsequent visions are John's first systematic treatment of *future* events and John emphasizes this fact. Whereas the preceding seven letters deal primarily with the *present* state of the church and only secondarily with the coming one, the visions from chapter six on deal almost solely with the future. Significantly, chapter 4 opens with the invitation, "Come up here, and I will show to you what must take place *after these things*" (Rev. 4:1).

Accordingly, chapters 4 and 5 would be an especially logical place for John to give us some clues about the ultimate basis of his predictions. As John paints the scene in which the sealed book concerning the future is first opened, he should give us some indication of how he can make sound predictions and how we can know he is right.

Naturally, if the clues we find in chapters 4 and 5 can be verified from other texts in Revelation, we can be especially confident that we have discovered the justification for John's bold prophecies. If important themes in chapters 4 and 5 also occur elsewhere, we can be sure these ideas are crucial to understanding John's thought.

Like other passages in Revelation, the scene in chapters 4 and 5 sweeps us away by the power of its kaleidoscopic images. As we move from the heavenly throne out to the twenty-four elders and the four living creatures and then back to the throne, as the Lamb comes and takes the scroll, as we hear the great choruses of praise, we are overwhelmed. The sights and sounds, the drama of opening the book are nearly hypnotic.

Nevertheless, literarily, the structure of the two chapters is simple and tight. Here is an outline:

An Outline of Revelation 4-5

I. Introduction Marking a New Section of the Book:
   The circumstances of the vision (4:1-2a).
II. The Glory and Worship of the One Seated on the Throne (i.e., God)
   (4:2b-11)
   A. God's Glory (4:2b-8a)
   B. The Worship of God
      1. The First Hymn (4:8b)
      2. A Middle Section (4:9-10)
      3. The Second Hymn (4:11)   '
III. The Challenge to Open the Scroll (5:1-4)
IV. The Glory and Worship of the Lamb (5:5-13)
   A. The Lamb's Glory: He alone can open the scroll and so he takes it
      (5:5-7).
   B. The Worship of the Lamb (5:8-12)
      1. Opening (5:8-9a)
      2. The First Hymn (5:9b-10)
      3. A Middle Section (5:11-12a)
      4. The Second Hymn (5:12b)
V. The Combined Worship of God and the Lamb with a Final Hymn
   (5:13-14)

As this structure makes clear, the basic theme of chapters 4 and 5 is that the *glory* of God and the Lamb is what makes it possible to open the scroll and know the future. The scroll appears at the center of the two-part vision (Rev. 5:1), and when we see the scroll we are confronted with the dramatic question, "Who is worthy to open the book and loose its seals?" (Rev. 5:2). John learns that no one is worthy, and he weeps much (Rev. 5:3-4). So difficult is it to take the scroll and make its contents known that no created thing is equal to the task. However, chapter 4 emphasizes the unspeakable glory of God. Therefore, we assume that it is because of this glory that God can know the future and so have the scroll and can give it to whom he will. Similarly, chapter 5 emphasizes the unspeakable glory of the Lamb and stresses that it is because of this glory that he — and he alone — can open the scroll.

Theologically, the vision in chapter 4 emphasizes that God's glory is qualitatively superior to any other. Revelation makes this point by discreetly refusing to describe the divine splendor. Whereas we have detailed depictions of the heavenly court, including the elders and the four living creatures, God himself is passed over in silence. We only read about what proceeds from the throne — "lightnings and voices and thunders" (Rev. 4:5) — for the one who sits upon the throne cannot be depicted in human language or seen with human eyes. Even the terse and enigmatic statement that the one who sat upon the throne was "like in appearance to a jasper stone and a carnelian" (Rev. 4:3) is probably not a description of God himself but only of the jewel-like radiance that surrounds him. Presumably John like other biblical authors thought that God himself had the outward form of a human being (cf. Gen. 1:26-27; Ez. 1:26; Rev. 5:7).

More specifically, chapter 4 emphasizes that the superior glory of God includes three attributes. First, God is eternal. Whereas all other things are created and, therefore, at least come into being, God is timeless. The first great hymn in chapter 4 proclaims he "was and is and is to come" (Rev. 4:8), and the subsequent verses stress that "He lives forever and ever" (Rev. 4:9, 4:10). It is worth noting that the phrase "who was and is and is to come" is almost certainly John's Greek adaptation of the "I am" that is the Divine Name God reveals to Moses in Exodus 3:14 and that is so prominent in the fourth Gospel (e.g., John 8:58). One of God's essential characteristics is that he is eternal. A second divine attribute that Revelation 4 emphasizes is that God is the omnipotent creator and sustainer of all things. He made all, and only by his permission do they continue to exist. The climax of the second great hymn is emphatic, "You created all things and through your will they existed and were created" (Rev. 4:11). The first hymn is equally emphatic: God is the "Lord," the "almighty" (Rev. 4:8). A final divine attribute that is stressed is that God is morally perfect. In the first great hymn the four living creatures proclaim three times that God is holy (Rev. 4:8), and in the second they say, "You are worthy" (Rev. 4:11).

Significantly, each of these three emphases in chapter 4 is also prominent elsewhere in Revelation. The eternity of God pervades the book; and the phrase "who is and was and is to come" already appears twice (!) in the introduction (Rev. 1:4, 1:8), and thereafter John gives us variations on it. We read that God is and was (Rev. 11:17, 16:5) and even that the Beast "was and is not and is about to ascend" (Rev. 17:8a; cf. 17:8b). Moreover, John has other phrases which stress that God is forever. God is "the alpha and the omega" (Rev. 1:8, 21:6, cf. 22:13), "the beginning and the end" (Rev. 21:6, cf. 22:13), the one who "lives for ever and ever" (Rev. 4:9, 10; 10:6).

The emphasis that God is the sole creator and sustainer of all things and is almighty also appears in various places. In 10:6 we are reminded that God created "the heaven . . . and the earth . . . and the sea," and a similar statement occurs in 14:7. "Almighty" is one of John's favorite descriptions of God and appears in Revelation's introduction (Rev. 1:8) and numerous other passages (Rev. 11:17, 15:3, 16:7, etc.). Moreover, it is always assumed that nothing can happen without God's permission. Even Satan and the Beast can do evil only thanks to God's temporary acquiescence (cf. e.g., Rev. 13:5, 7; 20:3).

Finally, the theme that God is worthy is everywhere presupposed. God is terrible in his holiness and visits judgment on anyone who works evil. Even the churches will suffer his righteous wrath unless they repent (e.g., Rev. 2:5).

Theologically, the emphases we have just isolated lead inexorably to the conclusion that in the end God will overcome all who oppose him. If God is eternal, then he will always be around to act. Whereas other things have their period of success and then inevitably pass away, perhaps "in a single hour" (e.g., Rev. 18:17), God endures forever and so will triumph in the end. If God is the creator and sustainer and is almighty, then in due course all things will accomplish his eternal purposes. Any rebellion will have to be transitory because finally nothing can escape the role for which it was made and kept in existence. Nothing can withstand God's omnipotence. If God is supremely holy and worthy, all will eventually have to acknowledge his superiority. To those who are open to repentance, God's goodness is an unavoidable challenge and summons. To those who refuse to repent, God's holiness is a consuming fire.

Accordingly, one important basis for Revelation's prophecy is God's nature as John experienced it and as his book allows us to experience it. In chapter 4, John invites us into a compelling vision of God's glory. In that vision we experience anew the truth that God is eternal; that God is the creator and sustainer of all; that God is holy. Then beginning with chapter 6 John shows us a vision of God suddenly making a final end to evil and challenges us to assent to this second vision. If we have assented to the first vision, we cannot reject the second. Once we have truly experienced the nature of God, we cannot deny that ultimately God will assert his lordship over all things and accomplish his righteous purpose and that God's triumph could take place at any moment he chooses.

If we now turn to the description of the Lamb's glory in chapter 5, we discover that it is the Lamb's worthiness that allows him to open the scroll. Whereas no one else "in heaven or on earth or underneath the earth" (Rev. 5:3) can open the scroll, the Lamb can. He can because he is uniquely worthy. The question with which John is confronted is who is "*worthy* to open the book" (Rev. 5:2). The two great hymns proclaim that it is the Lamb who is worthy and so can open the scroll (Rev. 5:9, 12).

Christ is worthy because of his sacrificial death on the cross. Here again the great hymns to the Lamb are informative. The first hymn tells us that the lamb is worthy because he "was slain" and "has purchased for God" by his blood "members of every tribe and tongue and people and nation" (Rev. 5:9). The second proclaims that the Lamb is worthy of "power and wealth and wisdom and might and honor and glory and blessing," because he was slain (Rev. 5:12).

Because of the worthiness of his sacrifice, the Lamb's death had three special consequences. First, his death led to his resurrection and empowerment. The Lamb we meet in chapter 5 has conquered death and reigns. He is alive forever and, as his seven horns and seven eyes symbolize (Rev. 5:6), he enjoys the fullness of knowledge and power. A crucial aspect of this power is authority over death. Since Jesus alone has risen from the dead, he alone offers to us a solution to death. A second consequence of the Lamb's death is that it led to his universal acclaim in heaven. Indeed, in chapters 4 and 5 Jesus enjoys the same praise as God himself. The two hymns to God in chapter 4 are paralleled by two hymns to the Lamb in chapter 5. Moreover, the final hymn in chapter 5 explicitly links God and the Lamb. Every created thing proclaims, "To him who sits on the throne and to the Lamb be blessing and honor and glory and power" (Rev. 5:13). A final consequence of the Lamb's death is that it has already begun his priestly kingdom on earth. By his sacrifice the Lamb has brought the church into being. The first hymn stresses that by his blood the Lamb has purchased people from "every tribe and tongue and people and nation" and made them "a kingdom and priests" (Rev. 5:9-10).

It is striking that these three themes all occur in the introduction to Revelation and so receive singular literary emphasis. The introduction states that through his death Jesus has become the ruler of all things. He is the "faithful witness who is the firstborn of the dead and the ruler of the kings of the earth" (Rev. 1:5). A few verses later John emphasizes that Jesus has authority over death. Indeed the Lord himself declares, "I have the keys of death and Hades" (Rev. 1:18). Jesus rightly enjoys praise from those who know God. "To him be glory and strength for ever" (Rev. 1:6). By his sacrificial death he has also freed his people on earth from their sins (Rev. 1:5) and made them "a kingdom" and "priests" (Rev. 1:6).

Significantly, in both chapter 5 and Revelation's introduction the celebration of what the Lamb has already accomplished by his death immediately leads to the forecast of his ultimate triumph over the forces of evil. Immediately after the hymns to the Lamb in chapter 5, the Lamb opens the seals, and destruction rains down on his enemies. Right after the acclamation of Jesus in 1:5-6 we dramatically see him returning to reign over a rebellious world, "Look! He is coming with the clouds . . . and all the tribes of the earth will mourn over him" (Rev. 1:7).

Theologically, this progression makes sense. The worthiness of the Lamb that was manifested in his death does guarantee that ultimately he will triumph. By his complete sacrifice he has definitively revealed God's love. Accordingly, despite the vicissitudes of this world's history, his stature will endure and his triumph is right. Because his triumph is right, God raised him from the dead and made him Lord in heaven. There his praise never ceases. Because his triumph is right, holy men and women confess him on earth despite the opposition of the rulers of this age. Christ's triumph in heaven over death and Satan and the continuance of his church on earth despite overwhelming opposition point forward to final victory. If even the power of death has been broken and even the rulers of this world have been successfully defied, then there can be no doubt that in the end the Lamb will be victorious over all his foes. If Christ alone has authority over death, then in the end he alone will determine who will have life.

Chapter 11

The Nature of Evil
and Our Hope of the New Jerusalem

A striking feature in Revelation is the parallelism between the descriptions of the Beast and those of God or Jesus. The Beast "was and is not and is about to ascend" (Rev. 17:8), whereas God is the "one who is and who was and is to come" (e.g., Rev. 1:4). The Beast has seven heads and ten horns; he also has ten diadems and a blasphemous name inscribed on his heads (Rev. 13:1). Christ too is symbolized as an animal, namely a Lamb, and as such has seven horns and seven eyes (Rev. 5:6). Alternatively, he is pictured as the personified Word of God, and in this guise he wears many diadems (Rev. 19:12) and has a name written on his thigh (Rev. 19:16). One of the Beast's heads had a deadly wound, but the wound was healed (Rev. 13:3, 12-14). The Lamb was slain (Rev. 5:6, 9, 12) and came to life again. The Beast "was and is not and will be present" (Rev. 17:8). Christ became dead and now lives for ever (Rev. 1:18).

The parallelism between the Beast and Christ was so important to John that it probably explains why John chose to make the Beast Nero and yet at the same time altered the Nero myth. When John wrote Revelation toward the end of Domitian's reign (81-96), Nero, who died in the year 68, was already a figure of a past generation. Probably the most important reason that John fastened on Nero was that it was easy to use Nero to produce a parody of Jesus' death and resurrection. After Nero's suicide, there were continuing rumors that he had not actually died and that he was in the East and would return with an army and conquer Rome. Of course, John basically took over this tradition, since Revelation has various references to an invasion from the East (especially, Rev. 9:13-19, 16:12-16) and states explicitly that the Beast will destroy the Great City (Rev. 17:16-18). Significantly, however, John altered the popular expectation in one respect. Instead of Nero remaining alive, he now rises from the dead. The only plausible explanation for this alteration is John's need to provide a foil for Jesus' resurrection.

If Revelation draws many parallels between the Beast and Christ or God, the parallels between Babylon and the New Jerusalem are no less numerous. In Greek the introductions to the two sections describing the cities are identical, "And one of the seven angels who had the seven bowls came and spoke with me saying, 'Come, I will show you' . . . and he led me away in the spirit (Rev. 17:1-3, 21:9-10). The conclusions to the two sections are also the same. In both an angel declares that what he has revealed is reliable, and John tries to worship him (Rev. 19:9-10, 22:6-9). The actual descriptions of the two cities have many similarities. Both cities are symbolized as lovers, one as a whore, one as a bride. Both are attached to an animal, the Whore to the Beast (Rev. 17:3), the Bride to the Lamb (Rev. 21:9). The Whore is decked with gold, precious stone, and pearls (Rev. 17:4), the Bride with transparent gold (Rev. 21:18), twelve foundations of precious stone (Rev. 21:19-20), and twelve gates, each made from a single pearl   (Rev. 21:21).

The parallelism that John makes between the Beast and God or Christ, or between Babylon and the New Jerusalem is both innovative and daring.   Within biblical tradition there was no precedent for picturing the forces of good and evil as alike. On the contrary, the Old Testament stresses the absolute difference between the Living God and idols or between the wise person and the fool.   These absolute distinctions in the Old Testament are theologically "safe," since they leave us in no possible doubt concerning the difference between good and evil and the wisdom of choosing the first. By acknowledging that in practice good and evil can look rather alike, John took a bold new step in biblical tradition.

Theologically, Revelation's parallelism suggests that evil beings always attempt to appear good and become most evil when the attempt comes closest to success. In his descriptions of the Beast and the Whore John pictures the very essence of evil. The Beast and the Whore are the primary tools of Satan and so are the very embodiment of evil itself. They also are the great instigators of evil in others. The Beast leads the whole world into idolatry (Rev. 13:7-8), and the Whore is the "mother of harlots" (Rev. 17:5). By picturing absolute evil as looking like absolute good, John suggests that evil by its very nature is a counterfeit of virtue. Evil is rebellion against God, and so the evil person attempts to replace God. Evil beings seek to obscure God's righteous judgments and replace them with some other standard. Of course, evil becomes most damaging when that replacement is the most seductive. The Beast as absolute evil explicitly sets himself up as God, and he is supremely dangerous because, thanks to the work of the "false prophet" (see below), he actually appears to be divine and supremely good, and so "all who dwell on earth" (Rev. 13:8) worship him.

Socially, Revelation's parallel descriptions of the forces of good and evil remind us that in John's context the emperor actually did appear to be the Almighty, and Rome did appear to be the Heavenly City. The emperors ruled over the civilized world as John knew it; they were held to be in some sense divine[1] and actually received worship. Moreover, John was fully aware that earthly power and prestige create an experience of the numinous. Indeed, he even concedes that when the imperial authorities make everyone worship the emperor's image, miracles can actually occur (Rev. 13:13). Power also creates a sense of worthiness. Power gives to those who possess it the ability to flaunt benefactions and clothe themselves with education and culture. Power inspires flattery from underlings. Rome was the capital of the empire. The city had a glory greater than any earthly rival and appeared to be eternal. John himself gives a magnificent tribute to her wealth and power (Rev. 18:11-19) and places in her own mouth the boast that she will never see sorrow (Rev. 18:7). His characters rightly ask, "Who is like the Great City?" (Rev. 18:18).

Accordingly, a pastoral problem John faced was how to convince his readers that powers that seemed so obviously almighty and supremely worthy were not. When the emperors were the object not only of endless flattery and praise but even of worship, how could John persuasively contend they were in fact evil? When Rome was the richest and most powerful city on earth and was already ancient, how could John persuasively contend she would soon collapse?

In response to this seeming power, Revelation points out that the Beast and the Whore are transitory, and, being transitory, they can collapse at any time. Only God and Christ and the salvation they offer are eternal. The empire and its capital, no matter how great they may be at present, cannot last indefinitely. Whereas God "is and was and is to come" (e.g., Rev. 1:4), the Beast "was and is not . . . and it going away to destruction" (Rev. 17:8). Whereas the New Jerusalem will last forever (Rev. 22:5), the destruction of Rome can come in a single day (Rev. 18:8).

In response to the seeming worthiness of the Beast, John stresses that the Beast only appears to be worthy because of social manipulation and is in fact a sordid tool of Satan. People are tempted to worship the Roman empire because the local authorities in Asia Minor glorify it. The world worships the image of the Beast from the Sea (i.e., the Roman emperors) only because the Beast from the Land (i.e., the local authorities in Asia Minor) gives spirit to it (Rev. 13:15). People believe that the Beast is good only because the local authorities appear to be trustworthy. The Beast from the Land has two horns like a lamb even though it speaks like a dragon (Rev. 13:11). In fact, however, the reason the local authorities and people in general worship the Beast is because of naked power and unspeakable tyranny. When people say, "Who is like the Beast?" all they are really saying is, "Who can fight against it?" (Rev. 13:4). People worship the beast because all who refuse are put to death (Rev. 13:15).

In the course of exposing the social manipulation that makes the emperors appear to be worthy, John presents a sophisticated model of the structures of oppression. According to the model, authority is delegated downward in exchange for worship that is promoted upward. Satan gives his authority to the Beast from the Sea (Rev. 13:4), and the Beast from the Sea in turn gives his authority to the Beast from the Land (Rev. 13:12). In return, the Beast from the Land makes everyone worship the Beast from the Sea (Rev. 13:12), and, when people worship the Beast from the Sea, they also in fact worship Satan (Rev. 13:4). A key support to this oppressive structure is that the bottommost member of the hierarchy appears to others to be good. The Beast from the Land has two horns like a lamb (Rev. 13:11) and can also be called the "false prophet" (Rev. 16:13; 19:20; 20:10). Interestingly enough, there is a suggestion in Revelation that the local authorities who deceive the faithful about the Beast may even include church leaders. Other than the Beast of the Land the only false prophet in Revelation is "Jezebel" (Rev. 2:20), who apparently is a leading person in the congregation at Thyatira. Significantly, Jezebel also seems to be counseling acquiescence to government authority, since John accuses her of promoting "fornication" (Rev. 2:20). Here "fornication" probably includes the worship of the emperor.

John's model for the structures of oppression fit his own situation well but seems even more appropriate for our century. In first-century Asia Minor the local elite aggressively promoted the worship of the emperor in return for economic and political concessions. The local authorities were Greek rather than Roman, and their Greek subjects trusted them. Consequently, the local leaders were in a better position to put moral pressure on the general population. It is, however, our own century that has provided the most striking parallels to the Beast. The totalitarian regimes of modern times, such as those of Hitler and Stalin, came closer to realizing John's nightmarish vision of demonic government than anything that existed in the first century. The worship of Hitler and Stalin and all the other recent megalomaniacs vastly exceeded anything that Domitian ever received. As in the first century, authority was delegated downward in exchange for worship. The government would give someone the authority to be a schoolteacher or a journalist. In exchange the person would agree to promote respect for the national leaders and their programs. Because the teacher appeared to be trustworthy, the students were deceived. Because the journalist seemed sincere, the readers believed. Moreover, in our own time the church was often willing to accept various privileges in return for promoting the worship of governmental authority. Of course, the acquiescence of the church was a significant factor in blinding the general populace to the real nature of the system under which they lived.

If it was only thanks to social manipulation that the emperor looked worthy, it was also only thanks to social manipulation that Rome looked glorious. John stresses that Rome appears splendid only because of its outer facade and that this facade is corrupting and based on oppression. Yes, Rome is adorned with marble and ivory (cf. Rev. 18:12) and graced with splendid crafts and music (cf. Rev. 18:22). However, the wealth of the city bespeaks her sensuality and decadence (Rev. 18:3) and makes her unspeakably arrogant (Rev. 18:7). By her riches she has corrupted merchants throughout the world and spawned a huge economic network to provide herself with ostentatious luxuries (Rev. 18:9-19). Moreover, the city oppresses the righteous, and her wealth depends on violence and slavery. Not only "in her is found the blood of the prophets and saints," but even "the blood of all who are slain on earth" (Rev. 18:24). John concludes his list of the shameful luxuries Rome possesses with the sinister climax "and the bodies and souls of human beings" (Rev. 18:13). The word I translated "bodies" also means "slaves" and, significantly, slaves viewed as objects rather than spiritual beings. Once one sees through the facade, the Great City appears unspeakably ugly.

As in the case of Revelation's portrait of the emperor, John's treatment of Rome was appropriate for his day but even more appropriate for subsequent Christian history. In the first century Rome was indeed splendid. Not only was she the richest and most magnificent city in John's world, she was the patron of the arts and philosophy. Nevertheless, she was also decadent and arrogant, and her splendor depended on military conquest and mass enslavement. In subsequent history various Christian societies have fallen into the same paradox of magnificence based on evil. For example, from the seventeenth through the nineteenth centuries Christian Europe achieved a grandeur perhaps never previously attained in world history. This grandeur included not only material wealth but also an outpouring of great music and painting. This same Europe was addicted to ostentatious luxuries and so did not hesitate to disrupt whole cultures in order to obtain furs and diamonds. Moreover, much of the West's wealth was based on the colonial conquest and the enslavement and exploitation of various groups including Africans and Native Americans. Revelation provides us with a timely reminder that we must look behind the social facade. We must not be so awed by the externals of a social system that we ask no probing questions.   On the contrary, we should see whether much of what appears to be lovely is in fact trivial, and inquire who is paying for the pleasures others enjoy.

A final way that Revelation unmasks the Roman system is by juxtaposing it with the glory of the unseen God and of the Jerusalem that is to come. The parallelism between the Beast and Christ or between Babylon and the New Jerusalem is an *ascending* parallelism. When John emphasizes a similarity between the forces of good and those of evil, the common feature is nevertheless better in the former. Babylon and Jerusalem are both adorned with gold, but the gold of Jerusalem is also as clear as glass. Babylon and Jerusalem are both decked with precious stones and pearls, but in Jerusalem the precious stones are the very foundations of the city wall, and the pearls make up the gates. The Beast and the Whore seem glorious only because in this evil age nothing more splendid is visible. John reveals to us the risen Christ and the coming Jerusalem in order that we may have a better standard. In comparison, even the best features of imperial Rome become unspeakably tawdry.

Literally, the climax of Revelation is the magnificent description of the New Jerusalem (Rev. 21:1-22:5). This description is the last sustained passage in the book, and it surpasses all the others in power.

This climax is anticipated throughout the previous chapters. In the seven letters to the churches we repeatedly receive promises that will find their fulfillment in this final vision. The letter to the church at Philadelphia proclaims that God will write on those who conquer "the name of the city of my God, the new Jerusalem" (Rev. 3:12), and the letter to the church at Ephesus promises that those who conquer will be able "to eat from the tree of life which is in the paradise of God" (Rev. 2:7) — a promise that we see fulfilled in 22:2 when we get a glimpse of the tree of life in the midst of the City. At various other places in Revelation we get previews of the resurrected saints ecstatically worshipping God and the Lamb before the throne. For example, in 7:9-17 we see a multitude that "no one could number" (Rev. 7:9) who "had come out of the great persecution" (Rev. 7:14) "standing before the throne" (Rev. 7:9) of God and the Lamb and worshipping them. However, it is only when we get to chapters 21 and 22 that we have a sustained depiction of the consummation that is hinted at earlier.

Theologically, the section about the New Jerusalem and the earlier material that anticipates it makes the point that if we are faithful to God, our reward will be true life. The City is the place where we will be totally alive. It is the one refuge from the "second death" (Rev. 21:8). In the City we may eat from the tree of life, which bears twelve kinds of fruit and whose leaves are for healing (Rev. 22:2). There we may drink from the water of life, which flows "from the throne of God and of the Lamb" (Rev. 22:1).

Part of this true life is the realization of all the ancient, unfulfilled longings of God's people and the abolition of everything that is wrong. In the New Jerusalem everything that was once lost is restored. The tree of life from which our first ancestors were exiled is there (Rev. 22:2). So are the northern tribes of Israel that disappeared from history long ago (Rev. 21:12; cf. 7:4-8); so are the twelve apostles of the Lamb (Rev. 21:14). In the City, God "will wipe away every tear;" there will be "no mourning or weeping or pain" (Rev. 21:4); there will be nothing accursed (Rev. 22:3); there will be no one who is evil (Rev. 21:27).

Another part of this new and more vibrant life will be the honoring and transforming of the past spiritual achievements of God's people. The names of the twelve apostles are inscribed on the city's foundations (Rev. 21:14) and the names of the twelve tribes of Israel over the gates (Rev. 21:12). Nevertheless, the glory of the New Jerusalem infinitely surpasses anything earthly Israel or the earthly apostles accomplished.

In the new heaven and earth no righteous deed is forgotten. Yet the trauma and suffering that often accompanied those deeds is no more. It is a joy to recall the pain of the past, and what was once bitter humiliation and disgrace has now become beautiful. The works of the martyrs accompany them; yet the martyrs have rest (Rev. 14:13). The Lamb's heavenly bride is clothed with the "righteous deeds of the saints" (Rev. 19:7-8).

In the city we will inhabit a universe where the glory of God transfigures all things. The universe where the New Jerusalem is found is not the one we know but a new heaven and earth (Rev. 21:1). In this new order of reality there is no tension between the presence of God and the existence of other things. God's presence does not minister destruction or death as it so often does in the Old Testament; nor do created things block our view of him, as they tend to in this life. Instead, God's presence fills all things and both affirms their uniqueness and realizes their potential. In the New Jerusalem God is the light, and all things are transparent. God is the sole source of illumination, and there is "no need of sun or moon" (Rev. 21:23). The City is composed of translucent materials, of gold that is as transparent as glass (Rev. 21:18) and jasper that is clear as crystal (Rev. 21:11). Hence, all things shine with his radiance. Like the Holy of Holies in the Jerusalem temple (I Kings 6:20), the New Jerusalem is a perfect cube (Rev. 21:16), because it was created to be the dwelling place of God, and his glory fills it completely. Consequently, the City has no need of a temple (Rev. 21:22).

In the New Jerusalem we will enjoy perfect human fellowship. Instead of resorting to the image of a garden, John pictures paradise as a city. Paradise is a community of persons. God and the Lamb dwell in the midst of their people, and so salvation involves being part of a holy fellowship. This fellowship contains people of every nation and is a place where the alienation between different groups will be overcome. John tells us the "kings of the earth will bring their glory" into the City (Rev. 21:24), and the leaves of the tree of life are for "the healing of the nations" (Rev. 22:2).

The most important aspect of the richer life that John prophesies, however, is entering into final ecstatic communion with God. At the consummation the God who is now mysterious and distant will become fully known and infinitely close, and we will be perfectly united with him. The Lamb will marry the Bride (Rev. 19:7-9). John uses various images to try to convey some sense of what this communion will be like. We will worship God and see his face (Rev. 22:3-4). His name will be on our foreheads (Rev. 22:4). He will be our God, and we will be his sons and daughters (Rev. 21:7). He will be our God, and we will be his people (Rev. 21:3).

Best of all, this new life will last to all eternity. In contrast to earthly life which is always transitory and can end at any moment, our final life with God has no limit. In the New Jerusalem "death will be no more" (Rev. 21:4), and we shall live for ever and ever (Rev. 22:5).

To bring the maximum impact of this vision of true life to the reader John uses all the resources of allusive language and symbol. He evokes the biblical heritage with references to the glories of the past such as the tree of life and the twelve tribes and with references to the unfulfilled prophecies of salvation such as Isaiah's promise of a new heaven and earth (Rev. 21:1; Isa. 65:17, 66:22). He draws on the most extravagant metaphors and images. The foundations of the city wall are twelve different kinds of gems; the city gates are pearls; the city itself is made of pure gold that is as transparent as crystal.

John's goal is to make this vision so compelling that we will be able to affirm that this is our ultimate hope. He wants us to be so overwhelmed by the beauty and profundity of his own hope that we will adopt it as ours. Or perhaps better: We will recognize that this is the fulfillment for which we have always longed and waited but which we never understood so clearly.

Of course, if we are able to affirm that the New Jerusalem is our ultimate hope, then we will be able to turn our backs on the Whore and suffer for the sake of the Lamb. If we recognize that our most fundamental desire and expectation is the true life that can only come from ecstatic communion with God, then we will not be beguiled by the tawdry consolations of Babylon. Instead, we will see clearly that Babylon offers only counterfeit salvation. We will also realize that the salvation God offers is so wonderful and so necessary to us that no sacrifice is too great in order to obtain it.

A key philosophic assumption that I believe John makes is that our deepest hope is an indication of ultimate reality. By painting for us a vision of ultimate fulfillment and then inviting us to assent to that vision, Revelation implies that our highest longings must be capable of fulfillment. Accordingly, what we desire most deeply should be an indication of what can finally be.

Personally, I believe this philosophical assumption is valid. We cannot discover ultimate reality primarily by reason, because reason only tells us about realities we have already experienced. We can think about something only when we have some data to consider. By contrast, hope can point beyond what we have already experienced and so indicate realities that are more profound than those we have so far encountered. Our most fundamental hopes must point us to ultimate possibilities. If they did not, the hope itself would be inexplicable. Just as the feeling of hunger proves that there must be such a thing as food, so the hope of true life proves that such life can finally be had.

However, often in order to recognize our hopes, someone must stimulate them by giving us a foretaste of their fulfillment, and this is what John does. Often we do not realize we are hungry until we catch the scent of food being prepared. So too, often we are unaware of our deepest hopes until we get some glimpse of their object. By giving us such a glimpse, John invites us to recognize our most fundamental longings and the divine realities toward which they point. In the climax of Revelation John describes the water of life (Rev. 22:1); then in the book's conclusion he invites those who are thirsty (Rev. 22:17) to wait for Christ to come (Rev. 22:20).

Notes

[1] I say "in some sense" because the emperors seem to have occupied an ambiguous position and never enjoyed complete equality with the gods. For a full discussion, see S. R. F. Price, *Rituals and Power: The Roman Imperial Cult in Asia Minor* (Cambridge: Cambridge University Press, 1984), passim.

Chapter 12

The Origin of John's Visions

In the last two chapters we have analyzed scenes from Revelation and emphasized their theological structure. We looked at such things as John's description of heavenly worship or of the Beast and the New Jerusalem. We analyzed such descriptions in order to get at underlying spiritual principles. The worship of God and the Lamb in Revelation imply certain doctrinal affirmations about them and the descriptions of the Beast and the New Jerusalem imply particular understandings of the mechanisms of oppression or the ultimate hope of human beings.

Such analysis is defensible as long as we think of Revelation as a theological document that makes use of literary patterns. If we hold that John is primarily concerned with setting out certain affirmations and that he uses literary techniques to present them as effectively as possible, then we can look for the basic principles that underlie the poetic descriptions.

Of course, much of Revelation is a theological work that employs literary techniques. In our previous analysis we saw that Revelation presents a basic message over and over and that the rich literary details are not meant to be taken literally. Their purpose is to dramatize the fundamental points John is making.

As we also noted, however, Revelation gives us a record of John's *visions*. John explicitly claims that he is passing on to us *what he saw* (Rev. 1:2, 22:8) and that much of what he passes on to us describes what happened while he was in the spirit. John writes under his own name to congregations he knows. Moreover, he attacks the credentials of an influential seer at Thyatira, who, according to John, merely "*calls* herself a prophetess" (Rev. 2:20). Consequently, his claim that he had actual visions must contain at least a fair amount of truth. Certainly, he could not have made such a declaration if it was wholly false.

Accordingly, we must ask whether, like John's literary techniques, visions primarily allow people to experience the power of underlying affirmations. In our previous analysis we assumed that the detailed images of Revelation are not important in themselves. Their importance lies in their ability to give greater impact to fundamental theological principles. Thus, the image of the New Jerusalem being made of transparent gold and translucent gems would not be significant if it were simply a statement about the chemical composition of the next world. What makes this image significant is that it gives compelling expression to a fundamental theological idea. The poetic image of transparent gold is powerfully moving and expresses the doctrinal affirmation that in heaven everything will be filled with God's glory.

Now we must see whether we can justify this approach in evaluating visions. Specifically, we must examine these questions: Is an authentic vision primarily a visible expression of a deeper truth? Can we reconstruct John's spiritual experience and how the book originated from it?

Logically, there are at least three possible positions on how visions originate and what they tell us. At one extreme, there is the position that visions come directly from God and give exact images of heavenly things. If someone has a vision in which the Virgin Mary is in heaven and is wearing a blue robe, then we may confidently conclude not only that the Virgin is in heaven but even that she is presently in a blue outfit. At the other extreme we have the position that visions come only from ourselves and so at most tell us about the working of our own minds. A vision is not a response to a divine impulse but to a human one. It tells us about our own fears, hopes, or pathologies. Thus, if someone says to us they had a vision of the Virgin Mary dressed in blue, we may conclude that the person comes from a Christian denomination that venerates Mary and has seen pictures in which the Virgin is in blue. We may also suspect the person has been drinking or had a nervous breakdown. However, we can conclude nothing about whether there is a heaven, whether the Virgin Mary is there, and whether she wears blue. Finally, there is the position that a vision is a culturally conditioned translation of a divine impulse. God is outside time and space and so divine realities in themselves cannot be directly envisioned. However, when the Divine touches the human, our minds respond by producing a translation into images or sounds that we can comprehend. Such images and sounds are culturally specific, because our contingent cultural background determines what symbols are meaningful to us. Thus, the divine impulse that inspires a vision is wordless and imageless; however, a modern American Roman Catholic might see the Virgin Mary dressed in blue who would speak in English.

In my opinion the first two models of how visions originate and, therefore, what we can learn from them, are inadequate for "authentic" visions. By an "authentic" vision I mean a vision that gives us a genuine experience of spiritual realities beyond ourselves. The first model cannot explain the diversity of authentic visions, and it also cheapens divine realities. Visions are a phenomenon that occurs in widely different times and places, and it is striking that the visions vary depending on the cultural setting. Catholics often see visions of the Virgin Mary; Protestants generally do not. Americans hear her in English, whereas other people hear her in other languages. Such variety is hard to explain if visions give us exact reproductions of heavenly things. Moreover, if we assume that visions give us exact reproductions of divine realities, those realities become tawdry. If Mary literally is wearing a blue robe or the gates of heaven literally consist of pearls, neither Mary nor heaven are all that splendid. By contrast, the second model for visions cannot explain the religious depth that authentic visions surely possess. No doubt, many visions are inauthentic. Often altered states of consciousness are due solely to natural causes, and so what we hear and see in them can rightly be dismissed as hallucinations. At most, they tell us something about ourselves. Yet, if we take seriously the profundity of certain visions and the positive impact they frequently have on human life, we cannot dismiss them as simply a product of our own imaginings. Yes, of course, every vision has a subjective element, and yes, spiritual experiences do tell us something about ourselves. Nevertheless, profound visions also have an objective content which tells us something about God.

By contrast, the third model for the origin and nature of visions avoids the problems of the other two and so seems to be true. If visions are a culturally conditioned translation, we need not be surprised by their historical diversity and need not cheapen divine realities. Each culture has its own contingent symbols, and so the translations of divine reality will be diverse and reflect the social background of the person having the vision. If a vision is only a translation, we need not assume that just because people see Mary in a blue robe, the Virgin is actually wearing one. Similarly, if authentic visions are translations of divine impulses, we need not dismiss the profundity of so much of humanity's religious experience. Beneath the culturally conditioned symbols there is a transcendent reality, and so visions do indeed tell us something about the Divine, not just something about ourselves.

If authentic visions are culturally conditioned translations of divine impulses, then a written account of visions can be said to be a translation of a translation. After the spiritual writer has the vision, he or she must then represent it in writing. Such representation always involves further alteration. To describe something we must single out those characteristics that seem most important, we must express them in the words available in our language, and we must place those words one after another. A sunset may be too detailed to describe exactly, too beautiful for human words to express adequately, and too unified for the sequential flow of language to do it justice. Nevertheless, if we are going to write a description at all, we must respect the limitations of human verbal expression. So too, a spiritual writer cannot transcribe a vision exactly but must translate it.

One of the great strengths of Revelation is that the author seems to realize that what he is giving us is a double translation. As we have seen, John appears to recognize that his predictions about the future rest upon his experiential awareness of the continuing nature of God and of the deeds of the Lamb. It is because John has experienced God's eternity that John can conclude that God will soon triumph. The one who is and who was is also the one who is to come. It is because John has experienced the power of Christ's love expressed on the cross that John can look forward to Christ's triumph. Moreover, John does not claim that his visions are directly from God. Instead, he freely admits they came to him through the mediation of an angel (Rev. 1:1). He also takes some pains to remind us that what we are reading is only a literary translation of what he experienced. Again and again he uses the words "like" and "as" to emphasize that what he has written does not fully convey what he saw and heard. Again and again he uses paradoxes to remind us that what we are reading cannot be taken literally. Thus, John tells us the radiance of the Holy City was "like" a most precious stone (Rev. 21:11) and the pure gold from which the city was made was as clear as glass (Rev. 21:18).

We can now attempt to sketch the spiritual process that led to the composition of Revelation. At a time in which the church was having difficulties in the present and facing the possibility of catastrophe in the near future, John had a series of encounters with God. In these John experienced anew God's nature and Jesus' worthiness and triumph over death, and the certainty that those who remain faithful to God and Jesus will be vindicated. Thanks to his cultural and religious heritage, this fundamental experience produced a series of visions whose primary content was that God would soon intervene to end the present age and judge the wicked and save the saints. Since John was steeped in the Old Testament, most of the actual images in his visions came from there. John then thought about these visions and translated them into written form. As he made this translation, he passed on to the readers both his fundamental experience of God and Jesus and the apocalyptic vision this experience inspired. In making this translation, John did not woodenly record what he saw and the principles that these visions expressed. Instead, he used a host of techniques to augment what he had seen so it would have the maximum impact on the reader. He organized his visions; he filled in gaps; he produced literary patterns; perhaps he composed whole scenes. He also added theological and social perspectives. He did all this so the reader would understand as clearly as possible the message of the visions, would feel the visions' emotional impact strongly, and would be moved to repentance and faithfulness.

We can confirm that our reconstruction of the spiritual process that led to the Apocalypse is correct by examining chapters 15-16. The opening of chapter 15 manifests exalted religious feeling. In 15:2-4 the glorified martyrs ecstatically sing God's praise. His works are "great and wonderful;" his ways are "righteous and true;" he is "almighty" and "king of the nations" (15:3). Then the martyrs go on to predict God's imminent triumph. Because God alone is holy "all the nations will come and worship" before him (Rev. 15:4). Immediately after the conclusion of the hymn John sees seven angels rain down final destruction on God's enemies (Rev. 15:5-16:21). Chapters 15-16 are tightly structured. The bowl visions fall into the familiar pattern of seven numbered pictures which portray the systematic destruction of the universe. After the introduction (Rev. 15:1-16:1), we see the decimation of the earth (Rev. 16:2), the sea (Rev. 16:3), the fresh waters (Rev. 16:4-7), and the sun (Rev. 16:8-9). Next we see the decimation of the kingdom of the Beast (Rev. 16:10-11) and the preparations for Armageddon (Rev. 16:12-16). Finally, we have the definitive destruction of the Great City and the world (Rev. 16:17-21). Because the material is so tightly structured we must assume that chapters 15-16 in their present form are an artificial literary creation and that it is at least possible that John invented the scene in its entirety.   Nevertheless, the scene bears witness to a fundamental spiritual experience of God's glory that in turn leads to visions of God destroying the wicked. We must assume John actually had this sort of experience, and it in turn gave birth to this sort of vision. On the basis of such an experience and such visions John composed the literary text that we have.

It remains for us to ask whether John's book is true. Now that we have analyzed the basic message of Revelation and the spiritual foundation of that message, we must pose systematically the question: Is Revelation true?

PART IV

Is Revelation True?

Chapter 13

How Do We Determine
Whether a Document is True?

The most important question one can ask about a biblical book is whether it is true. When all is said and done, other questions are only preparations for or consequences of this question and so become relatively unimportant if the answer is "no." Such scholarly inquiries as, "Who wrote the book? When? And where?" are useful primarily because they help us understand the book better. They presuppose that the book is *worth* understanding. Such typical questions as, "What is Paul telling us in this passage?" usually assume that what Paul is saying is significant. If we were to conclude that a biblical book is basically false and, therefore, worthless, all the other questions we customarily ask would become far less interesting.

Unfortunately, many Christians — including many scholars — do not handle the question of whether a biblical book is true very well. Conservatives often ask the question before crucial analysis is done, and they deal with the question defensively. They assume without sufficient investigation that biblical authors intended to describe what literally took place and that, therefore, the test of whether a biblical book is true is whether it is historically accurate. Thus, some conservatives assume that the author of Genesis primarily intended to give us accurate information about the beginnings of the world and, therefore, the question of whether the story of the Garden of Eden is true is primarily the question of whether there historically was an Adam and Eve and whether they ate a piece of fruit at the instigation of a talking snake. Having equated truth with historical accuracy, conservatives then labor to defend the historicity of seemingly unhistorical biblical accounts.

We can quickly see the fatal weakness of this conservative approach by considering the book of Jonah. Conservatives sometimes uncritically assume that the author of Jonah intended to give an accurate account of an actual series of events. They then labor to show that it is possible that once a man was swallowed by a great fish and managed to stay alive three days before being vomited up. The problem with this sort of analysis is that it takes for granted that the author of Jonah intended to write history. There is nothing in the text to justify this assumption. On the contrary, the text itself sounds more like a story or a fairy tale. If the text is in fact a story, then the author never intended to give us accurate information, and so, if we are interested in finding out whether the author's message is true, we will have to assess it on some other basis than factual accuracy.

In contrast to many conservative Christians, many liberal Christians pose the question of truth too late or not at all. Frequently, liberal commentaries spend their pages amassing data, and the issue of truth is dealt with perfunctorily, if at all. One reads hundreds of pages of scholarly minutiae concerning a book's historical setting or editorial history, and then the commentary ends. The commentator feels no obligation to tell us whether, say, John's Gospel is true. Often the commentary does not even bother to tell us what John's basic message is! Hence, we are left to our own devices, and sometimes it is by no means clear that the information we gained is helpful in assessing the book's spiritual worth.

I have structured this book so that we can deal with the question of Revelation's truth systematically. So far we have done the sort of analysis that conservatives sometimes neglect. We have looked at Revelation's historical setting, literary form, and visionary basis. Now it is time to do the analysis that liberals sometimes neglect. We must face the issue of Revelation's truth directly and at length.

In my opinion, to determine whether a text is true we must do three things: First, we must determine what sort of thing a text actually is. We must discover whether, for example, the text is a news report, a historical novel, or a fairy tale.

Second, we must determine what the proper criteria of truth are for the thing in question. Of course, the criteria for a news report, a historical novel, and a fairy tale would be very different. A news report is true only if it is factually accurate. What it says must have literally taken place. A historical novel need not be factually accurate to be true. Indeed, a novel is by definition fiction and so cannot record events that actually happened. Still, a historical novel must be *true to life*. It must present the sort of things that regularly did take place or at least could have taken place in the historical period in which the story is set. The characters and events in the book must resemble actual people and happenings in history. By contrast, a fairy tale need not even be true to life. In fact, by definition it cannot be. Still, there is a criterion for truth in fairy tales. To be true, a fairy tale must vindicate responsible moral and spiritual values. A fairy tale in which the wicked witch successfully killed the innocent young princess and then lived happily ever after would be false. Here it should be noted that in some respects the criterion for truth in a fairy tale is more rigorous than for truth in a newspaper article. A newspaper article need not vindicate our moral values. A journalistic report that a police officer got killed and the robber escaped with the money might be true.

The final step we must take to determine whether something is true is to apply the proper criterion to the thing in question. We must see whether the thing meets the appropriate standards. Is this particular newspaper column factually accurate? Does this particular fairy tale vindicate defensible moral values?

If we turn to Revelation, we can see at once that the book is at least two things: First, it is a visionary prophecy. Revelation records John's visions, and these visions forecast future events. Second, Revelation is an application of Christianity. Revelation is a self-consciously Christian work. The author interprets the message of Jesus and urges the readers to accept this interpretation and live by it. Thus, in the seven letters to the churches John claims to be writing messages from Jesus, and these messages make specific demands on the audience.

With a little reflection we can see that Revelation is something else, too, namely a work of art. It is, of course, difficult to define a "work of art" exactly and describe in detail how art differs from other things. Basically, however, art is anything in which form is a primary vehicle for conveying a message. In non-artistic works, form is incidental to what is being communicated, whereas in artistic works, form is central. Whether or not a diagram in a medical textbook is beautifully colored and attractively placed on the page is rather unimportant. As long as the information in it is clear and accurate, the diagram chart adequately communicates its message. By contrast, whether or not a painting is beautifully colored and has a striking composition largely determines whether the painting communicates. Even if the painting clearly and accurately portrays a scene, the picture will be worthless if the material is ugly and jumbled. The painting will not say anything to us if the form is bad. If communication through form is what distinguishes art, then

Revelation clearly is a work of art and, indeed, the purest example of art in the New Testament. More than any other New Testament book, Revelation's impact depends on its form. By itself, the *content* of Revelation would have little punch. As we have seen, the basic message of the book is simple and can be expressed briefly. What gives Revelation its stupendous power is not its literal content but its *form*. It is the evocative power of the individual images, the kaleidoscopic effect of piling those images together, the drama of the increasing destruction in the seals, trumpets, and bowls, and the haunting parallels between different sections that give the book its overwhelming impact.

Now that we have determined that Revelation is a visionary prophecy, an application of the message of Jesus, and a work of art, we must remind ourselves what the criteria of truth are for these diverse things and see how well Revelation meets them.

Chapter 14

The Truth of Revelation as a Visionary Prophecy

As we saw in chapters 3 and 4, there are five ways of interpreting a visionary prophecy, and they have different criteria for truth. Those ways are the futuristic, the historical, the exhortative, the idealistic, and the preterite. Here I will assume a knowledge of what these options are and will discuss them in a different order. Readers who do not remember chapters 3-4 in detail may wish to refer back to them. According to the preterite perspective, the "meaning" of a prophecy is what it meant at the time it was uttered. Hence, there is no objective basis for determining its "truth." Objectively, all we can determine is its original content. According to the historical perspective, a biblical prophecy was a prediction concerning the short-term future. Hence, the test of whether a biblical prediction is true is whether the forecast was actually fulfilled in subsequent historical events. According to an exhortative perspective, the goal of a biblical prophecy was to change behavior. The prophet predicted future catastrophe or blessedness in order to coax people into acting better. Indeed, sometimes biblical predictions were contingent. The prophet forecast what God would do unless people repented. Consequently, the test of whether a biblical prophecy is valuable is whether it has positively changed human behavior and whether it will continue to do so in the future. According to the idealistic perspective, a biblical prophecy is a specific application of a general theological principle. The biblical prophet began with a series of general principles such as, God loves the poor. Then on the basis of these principles and the signs of the times the prophet made specific forecasts. Because God loves the poor, and because Israel has oppressed them, God will destroy the nation. Since a prophecy is merely a specific application of a general truth, the primary criterion for whether a prophecy is true is whether the underlying theological principle is valid. The final way of interpreting a biblical prophecy is the futuristic. A biblical prophecy predicts events that are still to occur even from our latter-day perspective. Hence, the truth of a prophecy depends on whether it will be fulfilled in the years to come.

Although the preterite approach does not allow us to determine whether Revelation is true, it does at least tell us what Revelation originally meant and so we must begin with it. From a preterite perspective the basic message of Revelation in its setting is clear. John wrote during a period when opposition from the synagogue and pressure from the Roman imperial system was making it difficult to be faithful to Christianity. In response to this situation Revelation predicted that there would be growing cosmic disorder and governmental persecution that would soon culminate in cosmic collapse and a devastating attack on the church. Then God would suddenly intervene and alter fundamental reality. The dead would rise, and God would reward everyone in accordance with their works. Since this is what is soon to come, Christians should be steadfast and live in hope. Now is the time of testing and soon God will rescue us if only we remain faithful.

When we evaluate this prediction from a historical perspective, we can only conclude that much of Revelation is false. Clearly, many of Revelation's predictions were not fulfilled. In the years immediately following Revelation's publication there was no great series of natural catastrophes or, so far as we are aware, any serious persecution. Certainly there was no cosmic collapse or devastating attack on Christianity. The world did not end; the church on earth was not decimated.

Still, something striking did occur in the short run: The Emperor Domitian was assassinated and discredited and, as a result, the threat of persecution dramatically subsided. Unfortunately, our knowledge of the changing historical situation is limited. Nevertheless, as was explained earlier (in chapter 6), there were plots against Domitian. Consequently, especially toward the end of his reign, the emperor became fearful and began executing people on the suspicion of disloyalty. Under such circumstances, local officials in Asia Minor were understandably anxious to prove their devotion, and a good way to do so was to be zealous in promoting the worship of Domitian and his deified father and brother. Of course, such local promotion of emperor worship put pressure on Christians to compromise. A particularly difficult moment must have been the dedication of the temple to Domitian and his relatives in Ephesus. Under such circumstances John's prediction of increasing hardship and then catastrophe was by no means unreasonable. As we know, in the next couple of centuries the catastrophic imperial persecutions John feared became a grim reality. However, apparently when Domitian was assassinated, the danger temporarily eased. After his death, there was a reaction against him. His images were thrown down and his decrees erased, and historians such as Suetonius damned his memory. The new dynasty was more secure and seems to have downplayed emperor worship. Perhaps because of this new policy we hear nothing more about persecution in Asia Minor until the year 112 when Pliny, the governor of Bithynia, conducted a half-hearted local repression.

If something striking occurred in the short run, something striking also occurred in the long run, namely, the triumph of the church over the persecuting pagan empire. In the two centuries following the writing of Revelation the church grew despite the vicious efforts of the empire to stamp it out. Then after the conversion of the Emperor Constantine, Christianity became the religion of the emperors themselves.

In part the assassination of Domitian and the reduction in pressure on the church in the short run and the triumph of the church in the long run did fulfill John's basic prophecy. At the most basic level, John had predicted that soon God would suddenly destroy the church's enemies and put them in perpetual disgrace; God would save his people and the saints would reign on earth. And so it was. Suddenly Domitian was killed and discredited, and the threat that hung over the Christian community disappeared. Then, in time, the church did overcome the fierce opposition from the rulers of that age.

It should be noted that a biblical prophecy can be considered fulfilled if those who believed the prophet and acted in faith were vindicated. Biblical prophecy was not crystal ball gazing or horoscope reading. The prophet's primary goal was not to provide intriguing information about upcoming events to people who believed in the occult. Instead, the prophet's primary goal was to change present moral and spiritual behavior. In calling for this change the prophet did predict the future, and the basic prediction was always the same: Those who heed my words and do God's will are going to be blessed and shall, from the perspective of a later time, be seen as part of God's continuing work in history. Therefore, choose life by doing what is right. Because biblical prophecy was primarily concerned with motivating people to change their behavior, its fulfillment in detail was relatively unimportant. Whether God punished people by sending a flood or a drought made little difference. Often prophetic promises or warnings were vague. When the predictions were more specific, they generally came from the prophet's attempt to read the political or social signs of the times. The prophet noticed the rising power of Assyria and then assumed that this nation would be the instrument of God's judgment. However, whether this forecast was fulfilled exactly was not very significant. What mattered was that those who heeded the prophet's warning and did what was right despite the risk ended up being vindicated somehow.

From this perspective, Revelation's historical prediction was fulfilled. Those who took the risk of refusing to participate in imperial worship were vindicated. Suddenly, Domitian was dead and disgraced, the pressure to worship the emperors subsided, and those who had remained faithful to Christ were delivered. John asked his readers to risk their lives on the truth of his message. Those who did were saved and kept their spiritual integrity.

Like the prophetic books of the Old Testament, Revelation is an invitation to us to prophesy and a reminder that our own predictions probably will not be fulfilled in detail. In order to get people to act uprightly we should make predictions concerning people's future welfare and woe. The basic form of these predictions will always be the same: If you act uprightly you will *somehow* be blessed. Often our predictions will be general and vague. On occasion we will, on the basis of the signs of the times, make more specific predictions. We will say things like, "Unless we take serious steps to eliminate economic injustice, there will be debilitating class conflicts, including strikes and riots." Such predictions, no matter how perceptive, may not in the end be fulfilled in detail. It will be enough if people who heed our words and repent end up better off.

Let us now turn to a consideration as to whether Revelation is true from an idealistic perspective. The general principle on which Revelation is based is that the forces of good will triumph over tyrants who claim to be God. John's forecast of the Beast's sudden destruction and the vindication of those who refused to worship it was merely an application of this bigger perspective. The principle, of course, has deep roots in the Old Testament. The Old Testament emphasizes that God brings down the proud, that God judges evil rulers, that God destroys all that is idolatrous, that God vindicates those who are faithful to him. One of the strengths of Revelation is that it grounds the principle systematically. As we have seen, it explains to us convincingly why the destruction of megalomaniacs and the vindication of the faithful are inevitable. They are inevitable because God and Christ alone have real glory and worth; they alone are eternal and give the solution to death; and so forth. We have gone over these points in detail earlier (see chapters 10 and 11).

In evaluating the general principle that in the end God triumphs over tyrants, we must ask two questions: First, is the principle morally uplifting? Does the belief that God will finally destroy egoistic despots and vindicate those who resist them unto death actually inspire heroic acts and sustain hope in times of darkness? Second, does the principle usually generate correct predictions? Is it generally true that God, in the end, does unmask and eliminate wicked rulers and regimes, and if so, can we confidently predict that any given ruler or regime will be exposed and overthrown?

In my opinion the answer to both these questions is "yes." The belief that God will overthrow tyrants and vindicate those who resist does inspire people to suffer and die rather than compromise and does nourish hope, when to all outer appearances, there are no grounds for optimism. Similarly, it is the case that God does unmask and overthrow despots and their regimes, and we can use that principle to forecast the future. In the twentieth century we have had rulers and regimes who were more ruthless and idolatrous than any in John's day. Hitler and Stalin, to name just two, killed more people and received more worship than any Roman emperor could have even imagined. John's portrayal of demonic government is far more apt for our own era than his and seems uncannily prophetic. Yet, as John also prophesied, these rulers were exposed and their regimes destroyed. Moreover, their downfalls came for the reasons he emphasized: All human beings are mortal; real evil can only mask itself as good for a time. Even though Hitler and Stalin were long worshipped, today they are an execration, whereas those who died opposing Fascism and Stalinism are now venerated as martyrs. Moreover, on the basis of John's theology we may confidently predict the overthrow of present day regimes and the vindications of other martyrs. Today in China the hardline regime is firmly in power and the students who were slaughtered opposing it in Tiananmen Square are at least officially in disgrace. Yet it is most probable that in half a century the hardliners will be officially in disgrace, and there will be a monument to the students in the square where they perished.

We now turn to the question of whether Revelation's unfulfilled predictions will be fulfilled in the future. Of course, the time frame in which Revelation envisioned this fulfillment is long past. "Soon" (e.g., Rev. 1:1) is not two thousand years! Still, the basic question remains: May we continue to believe that the fundamental promises of the Apocalypse will one day be realized?

The basic futuristic message of Revelation is that the world will experience a particular consummation. We discussed the details of this vision earlier (see chapter 11), and so here a summary will suffice. The final consummation will fulfill history and yet transcend it. All that is radically evil will come to irremediable ruin. All that is good will be affirmed and transformed. The achievements and longings of God's people will be honored and realized. Yet the resulting state will be in a new heaven and earth that are radically different. The final fulfillment will involve living in a community where we all experience God directly and totally and where God's glory transfigures all things.

Strictly speaking, we cannot evaluate futuristic prophecy, since its truth depends on subsequent events. If we ask the narrow question of whether a particular prediction will actually be fulfilled, no one is able to give a definitive answer. Only the passage of time can resolve the issue.

Nevertheless, in the case of predictions concerning our ultimate destiny, we can at least ask whether they fit with what we have already experienced of the ultimate. Do they accord with what we know about God as he has revealed himself in Christ? Do they satisfy our deepest hope and offer us a plausible explanation of how such a hope could be realized? A basic philosophical assumption I make is that ultimately God will achieve his purposes. Since he is the creator and sustainer of everything and has already triumphantly begun his redemptive work in Christ, he will in the end certainly accomplish his plan for the world. Hence, from the present nature of God we can deduce the final state of the universe. Another assumption I make is that humanity's fundamental hope can be satisfied. If it could not be, we would not have it. As thirst implies the existence of water, so enduring hope for something implies the thing must exist. However, just because fundamental hope can be realized does not mean that every possible avenue toward it is equally promising. No, to discover which avenue is most likely, we must see which avenue is most plausible.

Because Revelation's prediction is in accord with what we know of God and does satisfy our deepest hope and most plausibly explains how that hope can be realized, I accept Revelation's predictions as futuristically true. The God of Jesus Christ is irrevocably opposed to evil. He longs to embrace all things with his love and bring them to final fulfillment. Human beings do hope for a transformed world in which evil and suffering and death are no more. We also yearn to see God face to face. These hopes have been expressed in story and song and religious treatise in various times and places, and they are certainly fundamental to my own life and the lives of people I know. It seems equally clear at this point in history that this hope will only be realized through God's power. By now it has become evident that neither technology or ideology will bring us to that consummation for which we long and for which we were created. Only God can do it, and only God will.

Finally, let us discuss briefly whether Revelation is true from an exhortative perspective: Has Revelation actually caused people to live better? From an exhortative perspective the heart of Revelation is chapters 2-3. It is in the letters to the seven churches that John directly criticizes the failings of his readers and makes his most explicit appeals for improvement. Each letter comments on the situation of a particular congregation and then gives exhortations. Moreover, John clearly intended for his comments to each church to be a warning to all because in every letter we read the words, "Hear what the Spirit is saying to the church*es*" (plural). Among the letters, the most important from a literary perspective is the last — the one to Laodicea (Rev. 3:14-22). As the final word of the Spirit to all the churches, this epistle makes John's climactic appeal for reformation and renewal. Significantly, the letter is the most condemnatory and yet offers perhaps the most moving promises. Unlike in any other letter, John's evaluation of the congregation at Laodicea is wholly negative. Jesus is so disgusted with the lukewarm Laodicean church that he is on the point of spitting it out (Rev. 3:15-16). Nevertheless, he promises that if only the members will repent he will come and eat with them, and they will sit with him on God's throne (Rev. 3:20-21). He makes this promise because of his love (Rev. 3:19), and he assures the congregation that he is standing at their door and knocking (Rev. 3:20). We do not know what impact this appeal had on the attitudes and actions of John's first readers. However, subsequently its influence has been incalculable. The condemnation of lukewarm Christianity has become famous. The image of Jesus standing at the door and knocking has been even more well-known. Illustrations of the text have adorned countless churches and homes, and the statement that

Jesus is "knocking at the door of your heart" has become a commonplace in appeals for Christian conversion. We must assume that a text which has played such a prominent role in appeals for change has, at least in many cases, actually produced the desired improvement. Consequently, we must conclude that from an exhortative perspective Revelation is indeed true.

Chapter 15

The Truth of Revelation as a Christian Document

Revelation explicitly claims to be a Christian work. The book begins by telling us that it is the "Revelation of Jesus Christ" (Rev. 1:1). A significant portion of the book—including the letters to the seven churches (Rev. 2-3)—consists of words that the heavenly Christ speaks. At various other places we see Christ being worshipped or smiting down the powers of evil. Moreover, even when Christ himself does not appear, we somehow sense that he is central to what is going on.

If Revelation explicitly claims to be a Christian work, then it also claims by implication that its basic message is at least compatible with that of Jesus. Christianity by definition is the religion that focuses on Christ. No matter how much different forms of it may add to Jesus' teaching, there is always the presupposition that we are also faithful to it.

Yet it is easy to get the impression that the teaching of Revelation is not true to that of Jesus. The Sermon on the Mount or the Parable of the Sower seem to belong to a different world from the seven seals or the Whore of Babylon. In part, of course, the sense of radical difference is due to different literary styles. Jesus used the simple images of daily Palestinian life, whereas John employed the kaleidoscopic and exotic images of his inner visions and of the apocalyptic tradition. In part, however, the sense of radical difference appears to be due to contrasting theological positions.

More specifically, two theological matters in Revelation's perspective seem to clash with that of the historical Jesus. First, Revelation is vindictive, whereas Jesus taught that we should love our enemies. In Revelation the martyred saints demand that God take vengeance on their enemies (Rev. 6:9-10), and later when God does destroy the Great City, the heavenly chorus shouts, "Alleluia . . . He has avenged the blood of his servants" (Rev. 19:1-2). By contrast the Jesus of history taught, "Love your enemies and pray for those who persecute you" (Matt. 5:44). The second respect in which Revelation appears to depart fundamentally from the teaching of Jesus is that Revelation seems preoccupied with the future whereas Jesus invited us to live in the present. Revelation gives riveting pictures of the joys and horrors of what is to come and warns us that there are signs that everything is about to happen soon. We are to live in reference to what is coming. Jesus told us not to take thought for the morrow (Matt. 6:34) and not to look for signs (Mark 8:12). The future will take care of itself.

Accordingly, we must test the truth of Revelation as a Christian work. Is Revelation basically true to the message of Jesus?

Basically, Jesus taught that we should think of God as our Father and so should love him and one another. A striking innovation Jesus made in the religion of his day was that he called God "Papa" ("Abba") and apparently invited other people to do the same. He taught us to think of God as someone who loves and forgives human beings. Hence, we are to live in confident trust in God and to love and forgive our brothers and sisters. The first and great commandment is to love God with all our heart; the second is to love our neighbor as ourselves.

Jesus proclaimed that through his own words and deeds the power of God was entering the world in a new way, overcoming evil and estrangement. Through his miracles the sick were being cured and the possessed were being freed. Through his preaching sinners were receiving the good news of forgiveness. In the movement he was beginning, Pharisees, prostitutes, zealots, and tax collectors were starting to eat at a common table.

At present, the new power is hidden, and so to benefit from it we must perceive it and make sacrifices, but if we do, we will subsequently reap a great reward. At present God's reign comes in quiet ways, and it is easy to overlook. To see it, we must perceive that an exorcism or the re-inclusion of a sinner is the very "finger of God" (Luke 11:20). Once we perceive that God's power has quietly come into our midst through Jesus, then we must sacrifice our security and surrender to his message. We must abandon our spiritual pride, our social isolation, our material wealth, and become like children. However, if we do, then in the end we will have incomparable wealth. Those who humble themselves will finally be exalted. The reign of God is like a treasure hidden in a field. To benefit we must discover the concealed treasure and sell what we have so we can buy what is supremely valuable. But if we do, the treasure will be ours (Matt. 13:44).

In the future the power of God will become manifest, but then it will come in judgment on those who did not repent and will lead to their exposure and exclusion. Soon God's might which is now hidden will break out. The kingdom of God will come in power, but when it does, it will be too late to repent. God will demand an account of all his servants. The secrets of every heart will be revealed. Then those who earlier could have heeded Jesus' words will be exposed and will be cast out of the holy community.

The great barrier to perceiving the kingdom now and so obtaining salvation is hypocrisy, and, consequently, hypocrisy must be attacked. Our inability to see is not due to a lack of information or intelligence. It is due to a fundamental rottenness deep within. Our hearts are corrupt and so prevent us from perceiving. Often those whose outward behavior seems most godly are most wicked within and so most unable to recognize the power of God at work. Hence, Jesus spent much of his energy exposing the hidden agendas of people, warning about the fatal dangers of self-deception, and calling for a transformation of our innermost selves.

Once one accepts the message of Jesus, one gains power to discover the signs of the times and so can determine the specific demands of love in a particular situation. Real goodness comes from a transformed heart. Just as hypocrisy can twist any legal requirement so that keeping it leads to evil rather than good, so real goodness naturally leads people to recognize what must be done in any given situation and to do it. A good tree brings forth good fruit, and a good person can discern what is going on in a particular context and what God is calling us to do in response.

In order to encourage people to uncover hypocrisy and discern the kingdom and the signs of the times, Jesus spoke obliquely. Rarely did Jesus speak in a straightforward manner. Instead, he preferred to talk in paradox and in parable. He preferred to make sayings that pointed in a certain direction but could not be taken literally. "If your eye causes you to sin, gouge it out!" (Mark 9:47). He delighted in telling odd stories like the one of a farmer who hired people at different times of the day and yet paid everyone the same (Matt. 20:1-16). The purpose of this strange manner of speaking was to shatter people's normal way of looking at things so that they could begin to notice the hidden sinfulness of humans and the hidden power of God in our midst.

Finally, Jesus taught that his own life was to be a pattern for that of his disciples. His conduct was an example for them to imitate. They were to live as he lived. His fate was a preview of theirs. They would share in his humiliation and exaltation. Whoever did God's will was Jesus' "brother and sister and mother" (Mark 3:35 and parallels).

If we compare the message of Revelation with that of Jesus, we see at once that Revelation faithfully attempts to discern the signs of the times and specify what the demands of God's love are in a particular situation. John looks at the inner condition of the church and at the larger social context and in the name of Christ issues specific exhortations. In view of the inner laxness of certain congregations repentance is necessary. In view of the threatening political situation congregations must prepare for the worst. Moreover, it is striking that John's exhortations presuppose Christ's love for us and demand that we love in return. In the introduction John reminds us that Christ "loved us and freed us from our sins by his blood" (Rev. 1:5). Then in the letters to the churches Christ rebukes Ephesus for abandoning its first love (Rev. 2:4) and promises the wayward congregation at Laodicea that if only they repent and open their door to him, he will come in and dine with them (Rev. 3:20).

Like Jesus, John assumes that in the present the power of God is hidden and so to benefit from it we must perceive it and make sacrifices, but if we do, we will subsequently reap a great reward. During this fallen age the powers of darkness overshadow those of God. In the church the backsliding congregation of Laodicea can confidently say, "I have become rich and have need of nothing" (Rev. 3:17), whereas the faithful congregation of Smyrna is experiencing "tribulation and poverty" (Rev. 2:9). In the larger world those who worship the beast will be spared, whereas those who refuse will be put to death. Accordingly, John must remind us that Christ has already made his people a kingdom of priests (Rev. 5:10) and that if we realize what Christ has done and make the necessary sacrifices, then we will soon reign on earth (Rev. 5:10) and inherit the New Jerusalem.

Like Jesus, Revelation proclaims that in the future God's power will be manifest, but then it will come in judgment and lead to exposure and exclusion for those who did not repent. "Every eye will see" Christ, but, as a result, "the tribes on earth will mourn" (Rev. 1:7). Indeed, John's essential message is that soon God will intervene in a drastic new way and destroy his enemies. He will expose the proud pretensions of unrepentant Babylon (Rome) and lay the city waste. He will destroy all who worshipped the Beast. Even Christians will be shut out of the New Jerusalem if they do not live up to their calling (e.g., Rev. 2:4-5).

Following Jesus' lead, John also sees hypocrisy as a great barrier to achieving salvation and so labors to reveal it. The Great City masquerades as beautiful and noble, and a Christian leader "calls herself a prophetess" (Rev. 2:20). However, John tears away the masks. The Great City is a whore drunk with blood, and the prophetess is a new Jezebel who is leading God's people astray (Rev. 2:20).

Like Jesus, John stresses that we must love God and that the only way to do so is to follow Christ. For Revelation, the greatest of sins is to fall into idolatry whether that idolatry involves eating meat sacrificed to idols (Rev. 2:20) or worshipping the Beast. We must worship God only, and the way we honor God is to be faithful to Jesus. Moreover, the greatest joy that will be ours in the New Jerusalem will be to see God and the Lamb face to face and have their names written on our foreheads (Rev. 22:4).

John, like Jesus, speaks obliquely in order to encourage people to learn discernment. The fact that John chooses a very different style of speaking obliquely than Jesus did should not blind us to the fact that the two persons share the conviction that normal ways of talking are not enough. Like Jesus' paradoxes and parables, John's visions by their very strangeness shatter our habitual ways of thinking and invite us to see with new eyes. John, like Jesus, hopes that as a result we will perceive the hypocrisy of this world and the hidden presence of God.

Finally, both Revelation and the Gospels teach that Christ's life is to be a pattern for that of his followers. They are to imitate his ethical example; they are to share both in his humiliation and exaltation. Jesus was the "faithful witness" (Rev. 1:5, 3:14) who willingly died. His followers are also to be "faithful unto death" (Rev. 2:10). Jesus sat down on his Father's throne and became ruler of the nations, and his loyal disciples will do the same (Rev. 3:21, 2:27-28).

As noted above, there is some truth in the claim that Jesus invites us to live in the present, whereas Revelation is preoccupied with the future, but the contrast should not be exaggerated. In the teaching of Jesus we are free to live in the present only because we know that God controls the future, and so things will turn out all right. We need not be anxious about tomorrow because God will feed and clothe us (Matt. 6:25-33). Moreover, Jesus looked forward to the destruction of the temple, and in the first three gospels he gives a series of predictions of future tribulation

(Mark 13 and parallel passages). As we noted above in chapter 8, these predictions provided a model for John's own visions. According to the teaching of John we focus on the future in order to live more responsibly today. John does not tell us about what is to come in order to satisfy our curiosity but in order to make us more faithful. He makes us think about the next age so we will not sin in this one.

Similarly, although Jesus preached love for enemies, whereas John rejoices in their destruction, here too the differences can be overstated. John leaves vengeance up to God. Indeed, by giving such lurid descriptions of God's judgment, John reminds us that vengeance is not our responsibility. Moreover, John insists that God's vengeance is just and unavoidable. God only destroys the unrepentant, and God's enemies are so wicked that even fearsome plagues are not enough to induce a change of heart (Rev. 9:20-21, 16:9-11). Because the wicked will never repent, the only way God can overcome evil is to destroy them, and they are without excuse. Hence, their destruction is right, and so the righteous are entitled to rejoice at it (cf. Rev. 16:5-7). In fairness to John one should also note that he was writing for Christians in an era of persecution, and so his vindictiveness is at least understandable. He did not address his book to Domitian and the imperial court, and he was not producing detached theology. He was writing for a community that was experiencing increasing pressure from the imperial system, and he was trying to rally people in the face of impending danger. Christians who do not live under such dire circumstances should hesitate to judge John's vindictiveness too harshly. We must also remember that Jesus too predicted that his enemies would come to destruction. His love for them did not prevent him from foretelling their doom. Those who rejected him and his message would, like a house built on the sand, fall into utter ruin (Matt. 7:26-27).

In conclusion, we may state that Revelation is true as a Christian work. Despite the enormous difference between the way Revelation presents its message and the way Jesus presented his, the actual messages are remarkably similar. John is right to claim that his book is a "revelation of Jesus Christ" (Rev. 1:1).

Chapter 16

The Truth of Revelation as a Work of Art

As we noted in chapter 13, the distinguishing feature of art is that it depends on form to communicate its message. In things which are not art, form is relatively unimportant and certainly does not determine whether the message is significant. The color and layout of a phone book or the cadences of an anatomy lecture do not determine their value. By contrast, in artistic works, how something is communicated is crucial and tends to determine whether something is really seen or heard. The color and layout of an oil painting are decisive, and a painting whose colors are pedestrian and whose layout is uninteresting will have little impact. Consequently, even if the painting's content in and of itself is important, that content will tend to go unnoticed.

To achieve formal excellence, the artist generally must depart from reality. The real world tends to be poor in form. Indeed, ordinary life whether in nature or society is formally chaotic. Natural vegetation tends to be jumbled instead of well arranged. People speak in prose, not poetry. Accordingly, the artist must rearrange and simplify. In portraying a natural scene a painter will present only selected elements and probably re-position them. He will reduce the undergrowth to a couple of brush strokes and place the birds in different groupings. Similarly, in portraying a character, a novelist will select only a few traits and make them more simple and transparent. She will make the character's motives easy to grasp.

Hence, art is seldom accurate in the strict sense, and so the test of whether a piece of art is true is not overall accuracy. Even pieces of art that we call "realistic" are usually very different from the realities portrayed. We generally do not mistake a portrait for a person. Moreover, some of the greatest representational art—and, therefore, some of the truest—differs radically from what it supposedly presents. Perhaps the greatest twentieth-century painting is Picasso's "Guernica," and yet, Picasso's scene is wildly "unrealistic." The contorted figures of people and animals are semi-abstract. Certainly one of the most influential political novels of recent times is George Orwell's *Animal Farm*. Yet the plot of *Animal Farm* is pure fantasy. In the book a set of animals takes over and runs a farm.

Precisely because art is not accurate, however, it is provocative and so causes us to look at the real world differently. If art were simply a duplication of experience, we would learn nothing. However, since art presents the world other than it actually is, art invites us to compare and contrast the representation with the reality. As a result, experiencing works of art leads us to reevaluate life. After looking at a portrait we notice things about a person's appearance we had not previously observed. After reading a novel, we perceive daily human behavior in a new light.

The test for whether a work of art is true is whether the work leads us to see the world more accurately and so allows us to live more wisely. Art that is false blinds us to reality and so encourages foolishness and irresponsibility. A television program that sanitizes war or a socialist novel that glorifies Stalinism is false because it keeps us from seeing important aspects of reality and responding appropriately. By contrast, Picasso's "Guernica" is true because its contorted figures help us to recognize the horror of modern weaponry, and Orwell's *Animal Farm* is true because its amusing events help us to recognize the hypocrisy of Soviet communism.

Generally, art helps us reevaluate reality by inviting us into an imaginary world from which we return and see the actual one with new eyes. When we see a painting or read a novel, we leave the everyday world and enter the artistic one. When a performance of Shakespeare's *Hamlet* begins, we enter Shakespeare's conception of medieval Denmark, and we remain there while the play lasts. At the end of the play we return home. However, our sojourn elsewhere gives us another perspective that makes us perceive our own world differently.

Revelation invites us to enter a world that is at once fantastic and ultimate. When we read the book we are part of a strange world. We see talking altars and transparent gold, many-horned beasts and bloody seas. We are also part of ultimate reality. We ascend into heaven and see the throne of God; we visit the New Jerusalem and behold the consummation of all things.

Artistically John's goal is to get us to see our present reality in the context of ultimate reality. He wants us to realize that from the perspective of heaven and of our final destiny, the rewards of sin and the cost of righteousness amount to little. In comparison with divine glory the power and the pride of the Beast are as nothing. From the perspective of the New Jerusalem the trappings of the Whore are tawdry and temporary. Of course, John's hope is that once we truly realize the relative worth of this age and the next, we will choose to suffer for Christ in order to obtain his blessings.

The question we must now pose is whether Revelation succeeds in this goal and so is true as a work of art. Does Revelation enable us to see the present world more clearly and, so, live more wisely?

In my opinion, if we read Revelation in the futuristic manner, the answer is surely, "No." If we emerge from the universe of Revelation and then try to correlate its events with headlines in the newspaper, we do indeed see our own world with new eyes and live differently. However, as a result we see things *less* accurately and live *more* foolishly. We see each major world crisis as a sign that the end of all things is near and conclude that there is no point going to college because the rapture will take place before we would graduate. As one surveys two millennia of disappointed hopes and wasted preparations, one has to conclude that Revelation is false if we use it to discern a series of upcoming events.

However, I believe that if we read Revelation as a disclosure of ultimate reality, we do start to see our own world more accurately and live more wisely. If we realize that Revelation discloses the final goal of human life and history and invites us to decide whether or not we will choose the New Jerusalem, then we do begin to perceive this present life differently and live more sensibly. Of course, each of us must answer for ourselves the question of whether Revelation enables us to see and live better. Accordingly, I will end this chapter on a personal note. Some years ago I went to a dramatization of Revelation. If I remember correctly, the script consisted only of the book itself. There were some visual effects, including dancing and strobe lights. On the whole, it is probably fair to say that the performance was second-rate. The cast were amateurs, and, perhaps due to a minimal budget, the special effects were only fair. Yet, seldom have I been as moved as I was by the last scene. When I was once again transported to the New Jerusalem and saw God face to face, I felt God's love in an extraordinary way and knew that this love was what I had always longed for and what I would one day actually experience fully if I remained faithful to it. Of course, when I returned to my everyday world at the end of the play, I took that profound experience with me.   I hope that, as a result, I have subsequently always seen my present circumstances at least a little more accurately and always lived at least a little more wisely.

PART V

Is Revelation Helpful?

Chapter 17

The Positive Contribution of Revelation to the Canon

In chapters 1 and 2 we noted that Revelation has caused problems in the history of the New Testament canon and the larger history of the church. There was more disagreement about whether Revelation should be in the canon than about any other book. As a result, it was the last document to gain general acceptance. Revelation has also caused an interminable series of predictions about when the world would end and so inspired widespread paranoia or messianic hope, and, at least so far, all these predictions have proven false.

Accordingly, if we are to affirm the value of this work, we must be able to point to major positive contributions that Revelation has made to the Bible and in the history of the church. If, following Jesus, we believe that it is "by their fruits" (Matt. 7:16) that we judge things, then we must be able to show that the Apocalypse has borne some good ones. The bad fruits are all too evident, and if we are to say that Revelation deserves its place in the New Testament, we must be able to identify crucial areas in which the book has made major contributions.

In this chapter we will consider whether the Apocalypse has made a useful difference in the New Testament canon itself. In the next we will turn to the impact of Revelation on Christian art and liturgy.

The Bible is a collection of early documents that became authoritative because they encapsulate the foundations of our faith. Thus, the Bible is first of all a collection of documents from the history of Israel and the early church. The collection is diverse and comes from many centuries. Still, one thing all these documents have in common is that from the perspective of church history they are all *early*. No biblical book is later than the first years of the second century. Moreover, in subsequent centuries when the church was determining what writings should be included, one important criterion was that biblical books had to come from the time of the apostles or earlier. Nevertheless, antiquity was not enough. Lots of ancient Jewish and Christian religious books did not get into the Bible. The books that did, did so because they came to be regarded as authoritative. Over the centuries Jewish and Christian communities found that reading and studying certain ancient documents was especially edifying. One reason for this was that these documents bore witness to the seminal insights and events that were the original basis of the faith. They provided a reference point as later generations struggled to deal with new situations and to set forth new ideas.

Because it encapsulates the foundations of the Christian faith, the Bible ought to include two contrasting qualities. On the one hand, it should be a unity and so give unity to our religion. The scriptures should not just be a jumble. If they are, they make the faith itself seem incoherent, and so do not give us a sense of identity or a foundation on which to build. On the other hand, the canon should also reflect the diversity of the faith and so be a helpful resource in diverse situations. From the beginning Christianity has contained many contrasting theological perspectives and social attitudes. In part these differences developed in response to different communal circumstances. Down through the centuries the church has continued to experience changing circumstances, and the diversity of scripture has been a vital resource in helping us adapt. The richness of scripture has allowed us to adjust to new conditions and at the same time hold on to our sense of being in continuity with the original traditions.

Revelation makes a vital contribution to the unity of the biblical writings. If we take the books of the Bible separately they are almost hopelessly diverse. It is not at all clear what the various canonical writings have in common, especially in the Old Testament. What perspectives do Leviticus, Amos, the Song of Songs, and Ecclesiastes share? A crucial unifying element within the Bible taken as a whole is salvation history. The Bible recounts the history of how God achieved his plan of salvation beginning with the creation of the world and of the first human beings. In the Bible the books are approximately arranged in historical order.[1] Genesis comes before Exodus, the gospels before the epistles. As a result, if one reads scripture cover to cover, there is something like a continuing narrative. Moreover, it is noteworthy that the Bible tends to place non-historical books in historical settings. The Psalms are often identified as "David's," the Song of Songs is described as "Solomon's," the tale of Jonah concerns a preaching mission to the historical city of Nineveh, and so forth. Revelation unifies the biblical narrative by bringing salvation history to its dramatic conclusion and so provides a fitting close to scripture. Revelation depicts the final events, and the book's concluding chapters give us a moving description of everlasting salvation. As the last book in the Bible, Revelation brings the whole scripture into literary coherence. The closing chapters of Revelation balance the opening chapters of Genesis. In Genesis 1-3 we have the creation of heaven and earth, the loss of the tree of life, and the first references to the serpent as an agent of evil. In Revelation 20-22 we have the final defeat of Satan whom Revelation identifies with the serpent (Rev. 20:1-10), the restoration of the tree of life (Rev. 22:2) and the creation of a new heaven and earth (Rev. 21:1). Hence, Revelation stresses that what was lost at the beginning of the Bible was restored at the end. The circle is closed. At the same time, however, Revelation also suggests that the Biblical narrative involves more than mere restoration. The New Jerusalem far surpasses Eden in splendor. What began in a garden ends in a city, and what started with just two people who fell, ends with countless multitudes of saved from every time and place and race. Hence, even as Revelation closes the circle of scripture, it also completes scripture's linear progression. God's plan which moves ever forward from its start has now reached the goal.

If Revelation gives vitally needed unity to the Bible as a whole, it also gives much needed diversity to the New Testament. Unlike the Old Testament, the New Testament—at least apart from Revelation—is basically uniform and so does not provide a rich enough expression of the breadth of Christian writing. Basically, the rest of the New Testament has only three literary forms, namely gospels, epistles, and the Acts of the Apostles. Accordingly, apart from Revelation all we have are retellings of the life of Jesus and the history of the early church and a series of pastoral letters. Revelation diversifies this literary structure by providing us with a Christian apocalypse. Similarly, apart from Revelation, the New Testament is rather matter-of-fact. We have straightforward and down-to-earth (pun intended!) presentations of history and doctrine. Revelation alone invites us to experience the evocative power of imaginative literary images. As a consequence, it is only in the Apocalypse that we have a sustained attempt to convey the glory of eternal life or the stupendous power of visionary experiences. Hence, the Apocalypse has been able to speak to many situations and persons that the rest of the New Testament does not address.

Significantly, Revelation provides a needed contrast to the relative lack of emphasis on loving God in the rest of the New Testament. Jesus taught that there are two central commandments — to love God will all the heart and to love our neighbors as ourselves — and he apparently felt that the first is even more crucial than the second (Mark 12:28-31 and parallels). Except for Revelation, however, the books of the New Testament place much more stress on loving one's neighbor. These books respond to a lack of charity within the church. Hence, they emphasize practical ethics. By contrast, Revelation is primarily concerned about loyalty to God. For John the issue is whether his readers will worship only the One God or whether they will acknowledge the blasphemous claim that a Roman emperor is divine. Hence, John stresses God's incomparable glory and the need for Christians to remain devoted to him alone.

It seems to me that Revelation's emphasis on loving God is especially needed in much of contemporary Western Christianity. The twentieth-century Western churches, in a laudable concern to address pressing social problems, have sometimes all but forgotten to glorify God and put him before all else. Instead of seeing loving our neighbors as a response to our devotion to God, we have seen serving others as the entire message of Christianity. To us, Revelation stands as an abiding warning that works of charity and mercy, while indispensable, are not enough. God himself must be the center of our individual and corporate lives.

Revelation also provides a helpful contrast to the relative lack of concern about political injustice in the other New Testament writings and so enables the church to resist oppression. Apart from Revelation the New Testament usually takes an uncritical view of unjust political leaders and governmental actions. Thus, in a too-celebrated passage, Paul claims that *all* political authority is from God, and, therefore, to resist political leaders is to resist God himself (Rom. 13:1-2). Similarly, even though Pontius Pilate as Roman governor tried Jesus and had him executed, the gospel writers exonerate him and, shockingly, transfer the blame onto the Jewish people and their leaders. Unfortunately, the New Testament's uncritical acceptance of governmental authorities and their actions has helped discourage Christian opposition to oppression and helped make the church an accomplice in various crimes. Happily, Revelation presents an alternative evaluation of oppressive political authority. In Revelation unjust political authority is instituted by Satan, not God, and the political leaders are clearly labelled as unambiguously evil. It is Satan who rouses up the Beast, and the Beast not only decimates the church but even blasphemes God (Rev. 13:6). Revelation insists that the only way to be true to God is to suffer and die rather than submit to political authorities who have deified themselves. As I tried to show in chapter 11, Revelation even has a complex and subtle analysis of how the structures of oppression interact with one another and deceive public opinion. Here we need only add that Revelation reminds Christians that our *monotheism* demands that we oppose social injustice. All too often Christians assume that the only theological bases for resisting oppression are God's love for all persons and Jesus' unjust execution. Far be it from me to deny that these are important reasons to oppose oppression. Revelation itself pointedly notes that God cares about his persecuted people (cf. Rev. 1:5), and Jesus was crucified in the "Great City" (Rev. 11:8). Nevertheless, Revelation primarily presents social injustice as a by-product of political idolatry. It is because Rome has deified her emperor and herself that she has become arrogant and feels no compunction about her lust for luxury and enslaving others. Building on Revelation's insight, we may add that whenever someone oppresses another human being, they have implicitly set themselves up as God over that person. Consequently, our Christian commitment to monotheism should lead us to resist oppression because ultimately every act of injustice is simultaneously an act of idolatry. Hence, Revelation provides us with a powerful New Testament resource to understand and to resist oppressive governments, and it is no wonder that Christian thinkers who have battled for social and political liberation have used this book to admonish and exhort.[2]

Notes

[1]By "historical order" I mean in the order that fits the historical claims of the documents. Whether or not Ruth is a reliable source of historical information, the book narrates events that purportedly occurred during the period of the Judges. Hence, in Christian Bibles, Ruth is placed next to Judges.

[2]For a recent and moving example of a book that uses Revelation as a resource in the struggle against oppression, see Allan A. Boesak, *Comfort and Protest: The Apocalypse from a South African Perspective* (Philadelphia: Westminster, 1987).

Chapter 18

The Contribution of Revelation
to Christian Art and Worship

Revelation has been an enormous blessing to the arts. Perhaps no book has provided as much subject matter on which artists continually draw. In the visual media, Revelation's gripping imagery has inspired and challenged Christian and even secular artists down through the centuries. Some of the major monuments of world art, such as Durer's wood cuts or the Van Eyck brothers' "Adoration of the Lamb" are illustrations of texts taken from the Apocalypse.[1] Even more significantly, Revelation has been a source for stereotypical representations and iconographic motifs. One thinks, for instance, of the standard image of the Virgin Mary as a woman standing on the moon, clothed with the sun, and surrounded with twelve stars, whom we meet in Revelation 12. Or one thinks of the standard symbols of the evangelists as a winged man, a winged lion, a winged ox, and a winged eagle, symbols that come from the four living creatures in Revelation 4. In addition to being a source for the visual arts, Revelation has also been a fruitful source for musical texts. Here again, both the high and popular levels of Christian culture are amply represented. For example, both the text of Handel's "Halleluiah Chorus" and of the ubiquitous hymn "Holy, Holy, Holy" are based on Revelation.

In the history of art, Revelation has spurred creativity and innovation. Particularly in the visual media, artists face the continuing temptation merely to copy what they see. Indeed, whole schools of painting and sculpture have restricted their efforts to giving accurate representations of the world as it is. Revelation, however, describes such things as a human being with eyes "like a flame of fire" and feet like "burnished bronze" (Rev. 1:14-15) or horses with lion heads (Rev. 9:17) and serpent tails (Rev. 9:19). These descriptions, of course, resemble nothing we encounter in the "real world." Consequently, down through the ages they forced even "realistic" artists to create something

fundamentally original. The aesthetic results have often been stunning.
Today Revelation's kaleidoscopic images should continue to encourage
highly imaginative and personal interpretations, as well as new artistic
styles and techniques.

Perhaps even more important, Revelation demonstrates that
images — not just ideas — can convey the presence of God, and so the arts
should play an important role in Christian life. Unfortunately, ever since
the Mosaic prohibition of images (Exod. 20:4-5, Deut. 5:8-9), there has
been a recurring anti-artistic bias in Semitic religion. The prejudice that
art — and, especially, visual art — cannot mediate God's presence has
repeatedly led to the suppression of religious painting and sculpture.
This suppression has been especially widespread in Judaism and Islam,
but Christianity has been by no means untouched. Iconoclasm in the
East and extreme Protestantism in the West have led to the exclusion of
art objects from worship or even their wholesale destruction in churches.
Even today the use of images to mediate the presence of the divine is
sometimes regarded as illegitimate. Revelation stands as a rebuke to any
such prejudice. In Revelation, God's being and attributes become
manifest through images, not concepts, and significantly the images are
primarily visual. We see God in the gem-colored light that proceeds
from his throne, or, as it were, reflected in the astounding things that
surround him, such as the four living creatures and the sea of glass (Rev.
4). Revelation's undeniable success in conveying the greatness of God
through visual imagery provides us with a powerful New Testament
warrant for the saving power of art.

Still, Revelation also reminds us that even great art cannot capture
God himself and should not presume to try. Despite the abuses that the
Mosaic prohibition of images has inspired, there is profound wisdom in
the commandment not to portray God himself. God exceeds anything
which we can imagine, let alone portray. Hence, when we attempt to
capture God in some artistic medium, we debase him and mislead
people. Visual images are especially dangerous because of the human
tendency to equate the visual with the real. For human beings, sight is
the primary sense, and, so, "seeing is believing" and "a picture is worth a
thousand words." Christianity teaches that when it comes to seeing God
in this age we must be content with the incarnation. Having forbidden
the making of images, God became a human being. Accordingly, for us
the face of Christ is the face of God (cf. II Cor. 4:6) and to have seen
Jesus is to have seen the Father (John 14:9). Significantly, Revelation

scrupulously respects the limits of art in this age. Despite his genius at creating powerful and evocative depictions of heavenly realities, John stops short of portraying God himself. When it comes to describing the One who sits upon the divine throne, John is content to give us a brief impression of the colored light (Rev. 4:3) and the tumultuous sounds (Rev. 4:5) that proceed from God's presence. God himself is passed over in silence. Instead, John reserves his first and perhaps grandest description of a heavenly being for the risen Christ. In the book's opening vision we encounter one who possesses the attributes of divinity. He is the first and last (Rev. 1:17) and the "living one" (Rev. 1:18). He has the keys of death (Rev. 1:18), and like God in Daniel, his hair is white as wool (Rev. 1:14; Dan. 7:9). Accordingly, John realizes that in this age the artist must be content to picture Christ. Only in the new heaven and earth will we see God (Rev. 22:3-5).

If Revelation has enriched Christian art, it has also enriched Christian worship. Texts taken out of the Apocalypse have had a profound impact on various liturgies down through the ages. For instance, in the services that my own Episcopal church now uses, many selections come directly from the Apocalypse. In our service of Morning Prayer, Revelation 21:3 ("Behold, the tabernacle of God is with human beings") is one of the possible opening sentences during the Christmas season, and Revelation 4:8 ("Holy, holy, holy, is the Lord God Almighty, who was and is and is to come!") is the opening sentence for Trinity Sunday. Two hymns from Revelation, "A Song to the Lamb" (Rev. 4:11; 5:9-10, 13) and "The Song of the Redeemed" (Rev. 15:3-4), are among the canticles that may be used after the lessons.[2]

As in the case of Christian art, however, what is even more important than Revelation's impact on specific works is that Revelation vindicates liturgy itself. Nowhere has the iconoclastic bias in some Christian communities had as profound an impact as on corporate worship. Especially in the more extreme forms of Protestantism, there has been a tendency to eliminate ceremony and reduce worship to extemporaneous prayer and listening to sermons. Revelation, however, portrays heavenly worship as full of grand ceremony. In heaven an angel offers incense from a golden censer (Rev. 8:3-4), the four living creatures never cease saying, "Holy, holy, holy" (Rev. 4:8), and the twenty-four elders continually fall down before God's throne (Rev. 4:10). If such is the worship God receives in heaven, one can only conclude that his worship on earth should be grand as well. Moreover, Revelation not only describes the glories of heavenly worship, it makes us part of them. Originally Revelation was intended to be read when each congregation gathered to celebrate the eucharist. The reading of Revelation was part of the celebration, and so John's descriptions of heavenly liturgy were a focal point for liturgy on earth. The earthly celebration became part of the heavenly one. In Revelation there is no separation between the worship on earth and in heaven. On the contrary, John tells us that all things on earth join in the heavenly worship of God and the Lamb (Rev. 5:13).

Notes

[1]A good collection of illustrations of the Apocalypse down through the ages can be found in Gilles Quispel, *The Secret Book of Revelation* (New York: McGraw-Hill, 1979).

[2]*The Book of Common Prayer* (The Church Hymnal Corporation and the Seabury Press, 1977), pp. 75, 77, 93, 94.

Chapter 19

The Value of Revelation
for Contemporary Spirituality

At present there seems to be increased interest in spirituality. Indeed, spirituality has become faddish. Seminaries seem to be offering more courses on prayer and meditation. In the church, prayer groups have been starting up or expanding. Outside the church there has been widespread interest in non-Christian forms of spiritual experience, such as Sufi mysticism or transcendental meditation.

In general this new interest in spiritual experience is a positive sign. It is encouraging that in the midst of a materialistic world people are becoming attracted to the inner life. One hopes that out of this interest there will be a rebirth of spiritual values and commitment.

Nevertheless, it seems to me that at least much of contemporary spirituality has two related problems. First, there is the problem of narcissism. The goal of contemporary prayer or meditation sometimes does not seem to be to die to self and become more given to the love and service of God and others. Instead, it seems to be to have esoteric experiences that one enjoys and about which one can feel self-consciously proud. Second, there is the problem of fragmentation. As we achieve increasing awareness of the complexity of spiritual experience, there is the risk that we may lose the unity of the spiritual life. We will become so preoccupied with categorizing states of consciousness or decoding various visionary symbols that we will lose our focus on God.

Theologically, the first problem appears to be due to a misunderstanding of the relationship between the Divine and created things. Spiritual narcissism presupposes that the individual is the center of reality and, hence, that experiences are primarily something we have. Accordingly, what we should seek is to possess the right ones and use them for self-aggrandizement. The spiritual sophisticate is the one who has achieved the "right" spiritual experiences and, as a result, exercises control over self and the world. By contrast, once we realize that God is the center of reality, then we also realize that we must live in total dependence on him. We seek to be spiritually passive so we can be totally receptive to the experiences God sends. Our hope is that these will be vehicles through which we give ourselves more completely to him. Such experience should lead to ecstasy — literally standing outside oneself.

Theologically, the problem of spiritual fragmentation seems to be due to a loss of practical monotheism. When we become preoccupied with states of consciousness, visionary symbols, angels, and the like, we in effect detach them from God. These things are no longer messengers and vehicles through whom we come to know God and journey to him. Instead, they become separate divine realities that are significant in their own right. In practice we have surrendered monotheism and embraced a polytheistic spirituality.

Of all the books in the Bible, Revelation is probably the one most consistently concerned with spirituality, and so it should provide us with a biblical perspective on such things as visions and ecstatic states. Unlike other biblical books, Revelation basically consists of nothing but visions. It gives us no narratives of a prophet's confrontations with human authorities or of a psalmist's personal difficulties or of Jesus' miracles. Instead, the entire work consists of spiritual experiences, and, as we have noted already, John not only tells us about his visions, he invites us to make them our own. Accordingly, if any biblical book should provide us with some normative perspectives on Christian spirituality, Revelation should.

Interestingly, when John wrote Revelation, the two spiritual problems we touched on above were appearing in his churches. At the end of the first century we see the beginnings of what would become full-blown Gnosticism in the second. People were increasingly aware that between the highest Divine Principle and human beings there is a complicated structure of intermediaries. People were also becoming convinced that these intermediaries should in their own right be the objects of study and worship. We may suppose that along with this functional polytheism there was the cultivation of esoteric experiences. Apparently, this proto-Gnosticism was becoming widespread in the churches of Western Asia Minor and John was concerned. The Epistle to the Colossians attacks the "worship of angels" (Col. 2:18), and it is noteworthy that the epistle apparently also was sent to Laodicea (Col.

4:15-16)—one of the seven churches that John explicitly addresses in Revelation. Revelation itself complains that in Thyatira some Christians study "the deep things of Satan" (Rev. 2:24).

Significantly, the spirituality John opposes seems to have had its experiential basis in visions. In condemning the worship of angels Colossians explicitly notes that the worship is based on what someone "has seen" (Col. 2:18). In attacking the "deep things of Satan" John indicates they are the teaching of "Jezebel" who "calls herself a prophetess" (Rev. 2:20). John also tells us that the two occasions on which he himself was tempted to worship an angel both occurred as a result of a vision (Rev. 19:10, 22:8-9).

In response to functional polytheism and the cultivation of esoteric experience, Revelation rejects the worship of angels. In the two scenes where John foolishly attempts to worship an angel, the angel rebukes him. The angel insists that as a heavenly messenger he is only a fellow servant and that God is the one to be worshipped (Rev. 19:10, 22:9).

In opposing the abuse of visionary material, however, John does not make the mistake of rejecting visions as a medium for knowing God, quite the contrary. Revelation itself is a series of visions, and perhaps nowhere else in spiritual writing are visions presented more powerfully. Indeed, the Apocalypse provides a fundamental New Testament warrant for the necessity of visions within the life of the church.

Strange to say, John does not even reject the existence and importance of spiritual intermediaries. In Revelation we have descriptions of all sorts of heavenly beings such as the four living creatures and the various angels. These descriptions are moving and fascinating in their own right. Moreover, as the various figures worship God or carry out his judgments, we cannot doubt that they play vital roles both in the adoration of the Divine and his governance of the world. The role of guardian angel is especially significant for the church. John does not hesitate to address the seven letters to the angels charged with the care of each congregation (Rev. 2:1,8, etc.) or to acknowledge that his own revelation came through an angel (Rev. 1:1; 22:6,16).

In describing his visions, however, John suggests that the fundamental Christian experience involves the joyful loss of self before the majesty of God and the risen Christ. In the apocalypse God is fearful and wonderful and endlessly fascinating. Consequently, those who worship him enter into ecstasy and give up all preoccupation with self. The four living creatures never cease saying "Holy, holy, holy" (Rev. 4:8), and the elders continually fall down before God in worship and cast their crowns in front of his throne (Rev. 4:10). When John is about to have a vision, he "enters into the spirit" (Rev. 1:10, 4:2, 17:3, 21:10), and while he is in the spirit, he is overwhelmed with the glory of what he sees. After beholding the risen Christ, John falls as if dead before his feet (Rev. 1:17). When no one is able to open the scroll, John bursts into tears (Rev. 5:3-4). Of course, when John describes his visions, we the readers also are so overwhelmed that we too lose consciousness of our selves and become fixated on the wonders being related.

Perhaps even more important, John's description of the heavenly beings never compromises monotheism. Despite the richness and power of his portrayal of such things as the four living creatures or the angel with the little scroll (Rev. 10:1ff.), the reader never sees these as appropriate objects for worship even if John himself is tempted to adoration. John produces this absolute subordination of heavenly beings by emphasizing three things. First, the glory of heavenly beings is only a reflection or a parody of the divine glory. The heavenly beings who are loyal to God only mirror the splendor of God himself. They have none of their own. Indeed, paradoxically, it is through the glory of the heavenly beings that we perceive God's own majesty. Thus, in chapter 4 John first mentions the One seated on the throne, but gives only the most fleeting description. It is as John describes the beings around the throne, the elders, the four living creatures, the seven spirits, that we begin to sense the splendor of the unseen God. Paradoxically, the cosmic forces who are in rebellion against God also unwittingly stress his glory. They do so by trying to achieve it and failing. As we saw in chapter 11, the superhuman forces of evil, Satan, the Beasts, and the Whore, are parodies of God and Christ and the New Jerusalem and in comparison with them become as nothing. Hence, ironically, the glory of the evil powers bears witness to the greater glory of God. John also relativizes the intermediary beings by making it clear that they are not to be worshipped. The intermediaries who are loyal to God lose themselves in worshipping him and carrying out his commandments and reject every attempt by John to worship them (Rev. 19:10, 22:9). Only the powers of darkness, Satan and the two Beasts, demand that human beings adore them (Rev. 13). The final way that John relativizes the role of heavenly beings is by insisting that their role as mediators between God and us is temporary. At the consummation Satan and the Beasts will be destroyed, and we will see God and the Lamb face to face.

In the spiritual life the key to overcoming narcissism and functional polytheism is praising God and Christ. Revelation has numerous scenes in which we glimpse heavenly worship. In them praise predominates, and the praise is always for the "One seated on the throne and the Lamb" (Rev. 5:13). The saints and angels never tire of proclaiming the greatness of God or the worthiness of Christ. As we read these doxologies, we too focus on the Creator and the Redeemer and lose all thought of ourselves and other things. The great hymns of praise in Revelation either come directly from liturgies in John's church or, perhaps more likely, closely imitate texts used in them. Apparently then, one message of Revelation is that in worship we must concentrate on praising God and Jesus, because such praise delivers us from preoccupation with self and enslavement to lesser gods.

Accordingly, it is evident that the Apocalypse has vital implications for the spirituality of our own day. In a time when we are rediscovering the importance of spiritual experience, Revelation is both an encouragement and a warning. It encourages us to be open to having visions and to take their contents seriously. However, it warns us that we are not to seek self-gratification or to become obsessed with symbols and states of consciousness or whatever else mediates the divine to us. Instead, we are to be open to the ecstasy that comes from being centered in God and are to keep looking toward him as the one to whom all the spiritual intermediaries bear witness. The path to such spiritual maturity is praise.

Chapter 20

The Positive Contribution of Revelation to Living in a World that Is in Danger of Destroying Itself

Prior to the twentieth century there was no danger that human beings would destroy the race, let alone the planet. Before the stupendous technological advances of our own era, humanity simply did not have the ability to wipe out civilization. At most, an evil ruler could destroy a nation or two. No one was in a position to destroy the earth.

With the recent scientific breakthroughs, such as the invention of nuclear weapons, however, it has not only become conceivable that human beings could destroy everything; it has become quite possible that we will. For a number of decades the capitalist and communist nations were engaged in a tense military standoff in which each side had the capacity for launching tens of thousands of nuclear weapons virtually on a moment's notice. Fortunately, with the end of the Cold War, the standoff is over, and the likelihood of imminent catastrophe has declined. Nevertheless, the long-term danger of nuclear disaster continues and, arguably, is increasing as more and more nations gain the necessary technology. Moreover, recently, there has been evidence that we may destroy the world by other means. For example, we are depleting the ozone layer that keeps out the sun's cosmic rays.

During the same century that gave us the ability to destroy ourselves, we also saw the worst tyrannies of human history so far. Prior to the twentieth century there were, of course, utterly despicable rulers and governments. Nevertheless, their destructiveness was tempered by a relatively primitive technology. It was most difficult — perhaps, impossible — to carry out the destruction of millions of people. By contrast, in our own time a series of ruthless leaders such as Hitler and Stalin have liquidated vast throngs and done so with surprising ease.

Consequently, the era in which we live feels in many ways like the period of tribulation that Revelation so powerfully describes. The nightmare of nuclear war or the destruction of the protective ozone layer have an eerie resemblance to the nightmarish battle scenes and ecological calamities in Revelation such as the blood flowing for three hundred kilometers (Rev. 14:20) or the sun gaining new power to scorch humanity (Rev. 16:8-9). The totalitarian governments of Nazi Germany or Stalinist Russia or various countries have an eerie resemblance to Revelation's description of the reign of the Beast (Rev. 13). Indeed, Revelation's descriptions seem far more appropriate to the horrors of our own epoch than to anything that occurred in John's day.

The uncanny parallels between John's prophetic vision and our own historical experience are not, however, due to John foreseeing the events of our time. As we have noted before, John did not make detailed predictions about coming occurrences. Moreover, what predictions he did make concerned the short-term future. Attempts to correlate Revelation's images with the events of our own century have been forced and have produced predictions that have not been fulfilled.

The eerie resemblance is due to the fact that John tried to describe the absolute and, as our technology has increased, we have come ever closer to being able to produce the absolute. John's visions concerned the ultimate — the final rebellion of Satan and the final destruction. Consequently, his visions came less from what his culture had experienced than from his own creative intuition concerning the worst that any culture could conceivably experience. John imagined what ultimate tyranny or what ultimate devastation would be like. Of course, as our technological capacities have skyrocketed, our ability actually to produce such nightmares has grown.

As Revelation's horrifying visions have increasingly been realized, Revelation has comforted Christians by providing us with a biblical name for the nameless. Psychologically, the unknown is always more frightening than the known. No matter how horrible something may be in actuality, it is always less horrible than what we can imagine. An important part of making something known is giving it a name. To give something a name is to put it in perspective. As soon as we know the name of some problem, we can at least discuss it and so can gain some mastery over it. To know the name of a demon is the first step to casting it out. Revelation has given us biblical names for the ultimate battle and the ultimate tyrant. The first is "Armageddon" (Rev. 16:16); the second is the "Beast." Significantly, at least the first term has been so useful that it has entered into ordinary English usage.

Revelation has given further comfort by assuring us that what it names cannot disrupt God's plan of salvation. Revelation insists that even the most horrible things that can be imagined, even the tyranny of the Beast or the Battle of Armageddon, do not negate God's providence. Indeed, these nightmares have been incorporated into God's plan and so in some sense can be said to be part of it. As we have dealt with totalitarian regimes and nuclear build-up, Revelation has assured us that ultimately God is in control and that regardless of what may happen in this life, there is eternal life. Amidst the horrors of our century, this assurance has been the one hope that has remained secure.

Significantly, this assurance has been a great benefit even to Revelation's most misinformed readers. Earlier I complained that attempts to identify one's enemy of the moment as the Beast or identify one's own time as the last days have been groundless and led to polarization and disappointment (see chapter 1). Nevertheless, even when people have misinterpreted the Apocalypse by trying to use it to decode current events, they profited from the book's basic affirmation. When people identified their most feared enemy as the anti-Christ or the most alarming military trends as the prelude to Armageddon, they could not help remembering Revelation's declaration that these too are ultimately under God's control and will not impede final salvation. Hence, even when Revelation is badly misunderstood, it remains a source of unconquerable hope.

From the perspective of social philosophy, Revelation reminds us that "progress" in human history is not necessary for history to be ultimately worthwhile and meaningful. In recent centuries there has been the widespread conviction that human beings are finally getting control over our problems and that therefore things are (or, at least, soon will be) getting better and better. Significantly, the conviction that civilization is moving forward has been popular among non-religious people. To them it provided the assurance that history was meaningful apart from any transcendent spiritual goal. Of course, in the face of totalitarianism and nuclear build-up, it was not always easy to maintain the belief that things were indeed getting better. One result was recurrent cynicism or despair about the human enterprise. In contrast to the secular perspective of "progress" Revelation offered the perspective that in the end things in this world would not get better but catastrophically worse.   Yet for Revelation this devolution did not necessitate either cynicism or despair. History has a transcendent goal, and no matter how terrible things may turn out in this age, God's will is being realized and salvation will surely come.

It is still too early to be certain whether progress or catastrophe will be victorious, but ironically if progress does prevail, it may do so because we have adopted the larger perspective of Revelation. Strange to say, often if we attribute too much importance to doing some small thing, we are unable to do it successfully.   If we think that passing an examination is crucial to our worth as a human being, then we panic during the test and are unable to pass.   Accordingly, often the way to accomplish small things is to realize their relative unimportance in the light of more fundamental matters. If we realize that God will love us regardless of whether we pass the examination, we will feel more secure while taking it and, as a result, will actually pass. Revelation suggests that progress in this age is not crucial.   What is crucial is that God is unspeakably glorious, that he has an eternal plan, and that that plan will be realized regardless of human evil. What is important is for us to focus on that plan. If we do, Revelation assures us that we will be able to endure whatever ill may occur in this transitory age, and in the end we will have eternal salvation. Could we take Revelation's logic one step further and argue that if we recognize the relative unimportance of this age then we will be less intimidated by its problems and so be better able to solve them? Could it be that the peace and hope that Revelation's message can give will enable us even to accomplish social goals in this life? Could it be that the only way we will be able to improve this world fundamentally will be to realize more deeply Revelation's vision that this life is only a prelude to final union with God in Christ?

Titles Available from BIBAL Press:

___ Ivan J. Ball, Jr., *A Rhetorical Study of Zephaniah* ISBN 0-941037-02-9 [$16.95]

___ Duane L. Christensen, ed., *Experiencing the Exodus* ISBN 0-941037-03-7 [$7.95]

___ Ronald E. Clements, *Wisdom for a Changing World: Wisdom in Old Testament Theology* ISBN 0-941037-13-4 [$7.95]

___ L. R. Elliott, *The Greek Verb System: Seven-Color Chart* ISBN 0-941037-11-8 [$3.50]

___ Suzanne Haïk-Vantoura, *The Music of the Bible Revealed* ISBN 0-941037-10-X[$29.95]

___ Norbert F. Lohfink, S.J., *Option for the Poor: The Basic Principle of Liberation Theology in the Light of the Bible* ISBN 0-941037-00-2 [$7.95]

___ A. Dean McKenzie, *Sacred Images and the Millennium: Christianity and Russia (A.D. 988-1988)* ISBN 0-941037-12-6 [$7.50]

___ Jo Milgrom, *The Binding of Isaac: The Akedah—A Primary Symbol in Jewish Thought and Art* ISBN 0-941037-05-3 [$16.95]

___ J. Dale Nystrom, *Bible Lands Resource: A Lifetime Bible Lands Companion* ISBN 0-941037-17-7 [$9.95]

___ William R. Scott, *A Simplified Guide to BHS (Biblia Hebraica Stuttgartensia)* ISBN 0-941037-14-2 [$6.95]

___ Robert J. St. Clair, *Prayers for People Like Me* ISBN 0-941037-09-6 [$6.95]

___ Robert J. St. Clair, *Co-Discovery: The Theory and Practice of Experiential Theology* ISBN 0-941037-25-8 [$12.95]

___ Scott Gambrill Sinclair, *Revelation—A Book for the Rest of Us* ISBN 0-941037-19-3 [$12.95]

___ Margery W. Terpstra, *Life is to Grow On: The ABC's of Holistic Growth* ISBN 0-941037-16-9 [$16.95]

BIBAL Monograph Series

___ 1 *Jesus Christ According to Paul: The Christologies of Paul's Undisputed Epistles and the Christology of Paul*, Scott Gambrill Sinclair ISBN 0-941037-08-8 [$12.95]

___ 2 *Enoch and Daniel: A Form Critical and Sociological Study of Historical Apocalypses* Stephen Breck Reid ISBN 0-941037-07-X [$12.95]

___ 3 *Prophecy and War in Ancient Israel: Studies in the Oracles Against the Nations* Duane L. Christensen ISBN 0-941037-06-1 [$14.95]

Publications in Process:

Guia para el Uso de la Biblia Hebraica Stuttgartensia, W. R. Scott (trans. E. Sánchez)
The Inerrancy of Scripture and Other Essays, Norbert F. Lohfink, S.J.
Reading New Testament Greek, Paul Danove and David Hester
The Stories of Genesis, Hermann Gunkel (trans. John J. Scullion, S.J.)
The Whole-Brain Bible: Resource Guide for Creative Teaching, Carole R. Fontaine, ed.

Shipping Schedule:	Up to $10	$2.25	
	$10-20	3.00	
Sales Tax 8¼%	$20-50	4.00	
(California residents only)	$50-100	5.50	
	$100+	6%	June 1992

Mail check or money order to: BIBAL Press, P.O. Box 11123
Berkeley, CA 94701-2123   510/799-9252   FAX 510/527-2823

[*Please Note*: Prices subject to change without notice]